FLOYD CLYMER'S MOTORCYCLIST'S LIBRARY

THE BOOK OF THE ROYAL ENFIELD

A COMPLETE GUIDE FOR OWNERS AND PROSPECTIVE PURCHASERS OF ROYAL ENFIELD MOTOR-CYCLES FROM 1934 ONWARDS

BY

"R. E. RYDER"

DEALING WITH EVERY PHASE OF THE SUBJECT, INCLUDING CHAPTERS ON DRIVING, LEGAL MATTERS, FIRST PRINCIPLES, LUBRICATION, ELECTRIC LIGHTING AND OVERHAULING

ANNOUNCEMENT

By special arrangement with the original publishers of this book, Sir Isaac Pitman & Son, Ltd., of London, England, we have secured the exclusive publishing rights for this book, as well as all others in THE MOTORCYCLIST'S LIBRARY.

Included in THE MOTORCYCLIST'S LIBRARY are complete instruction manuals covering the care and operation of respective motorcycles and engines; valuable data on speed tuning, and thrilling accounts of motorcycle race events. See listing of available titles elsewhere in this edition.

We consider it a privilege to be able to offer so many fine titles to our customers.

FLOYD CLYMER
Publisher of Books Pertaining to Automobiles and Motorcycles

2125 W. PICO ST.   LOS ANGELES 6, CALIF.

INTRODUCTION

Welcome to the world of digital publishing ~ the book you now hold in your hand, while unchanged from the original edition, was printed using the latest state of the art digital technology. The advent of print-on-demand has forever changed the publishing process, never has information been so accessible and it is our hope that this book serves your informational needs for years to come. If this is your first exposure to digital publishing, we hope that you are pleased with the results. Many more titles of interest to the classic automobile and motorcycle enthusiast, collector and restorer are available via our website at www.VelocePress.com. We hope that you find this title as interesting as we do.

NOTE FROM THE PUBLISHER

The information presented is true and complete to the best of our knowledge. All recommendations are made without any guarantees on the part of the author or the publisher, who also disclaim all liability incurred with the use of this information.

TRADEMARKS

We recognize that some words, model names and designations, for example, mentioned herein are the property of the trademark holder. We use them for identification purposes only. This is not an official publication.

INFORMATION ON THE USE OF THIS PUBLICATION

This manual is an invaluable resource for the classic motorcycle enthusiast and a "must have" for owners interested in performing their own maintenance. However, in today's information age we are constantly subject to changes in common practice, new technology, availability of improved materials and increased awareness of chemical toxicity. As such, it is advised that the user consult with an experienced professional prior to undertaking any procedure described herein. While every care has been taken to ensure correctness of information, it is obviously not possible to guarantee complete freedom from errors or omissions or to accept liability arising from such errors or omissions. Therefore, any individual that uses the information contained within, or elects to perform or participate in do-it-yourself repairs or modifications acknowledges that there is a risk factor involved and that the publisher or its associates cannot be held responsible for personal injury or property damage resulting from the use of the information or the outcome of such procedures.

WARNING!

One final word of advice, this publication is intended to be used as a reference guide, and when in doubt the reader should consult with a qualified technician.

PREFACE

THE purpose of this book is to provide the reader with such information as every motor-cyclist should possess; with, in addition, all that which is of a more particular and exclusive value to the owner, or prospective owner, of a Royal Enfield machine. Provided that its pages have been read and their contents assimilated, the reader may consider himself as qualified to take charge of a motor-cycle; in so far as knowledge, *per se*, constitutes a qualification. He—or she—will also be not only acquainted with motor-cycle matters in general, but will possess, further, a specialized knowledge of the Royal Enfield machine.

A handbook of this kind is meant not only to be read through, but to be kept for reference. It should be studied fully by the novice before he takes to the road, and certain chapters, notably those relating to driving and to road laws and usages, must be fully understood. Other sections, for example those dealing with adjustments and overhauling, will be found mainly of value for reference as occasion arises.

CONTENTS

CHAP.		PAGE
I.	THE ENFIELD RANGE	1
II.	DRIVING	9
III.	MECHANICAL FIRST PRINCIPLES	22
IV.	THE CARBURETTOR AND IGNITION	31
V.	ALL ABOUT LUBRICATION	51
VI.	CARE OF ELECTRICAL EQUIPMENT	69
VII.	ADJUSTMENTS AND OVERHAULING	86
	APPENDIX	121
	INDEX	130

BOOK OF
THE ROYAL ENFIELD

CHAPTER I

THE ENFIELD RANGE

Power Units. All engines except that of the passenger Model K are of the popular single-cylinder type. Detachable cylinder heads (of cast-iron on all engines) are provided except on the two-stroke model, to facilitate decarbonizing the piston which is diamond-turned from a special aluminium alloy which is carefully heat treated to prevent "growth" and to give the necessary degree of hardness. Fully floating gudgeon-pins of $\frac{5}{8}$ in. to $\frac{7}{8}$ in. diameter are used, and except on Models C and A, the two-stroke (copper end pads), wire circlips are employed to prevent the cylinder walls being scored. Connecting-rods are of steel of H section and have roller big-end bearings. Roller bearings (graded to 10,000th in.) are also used for the main shafts except on the two-stroke models. The flywheel assembly is exceptionally rigid, as is the crankcase in which it revolves.

Two camshafts are employed on all four-strokes and the cams directly actuate flat base tappets of large diameter. On the overhead-valve engines tubular steel push-rods are interposed between the tappets and valve rockers, and these are enclosed in a most ingenious and effective manner, the rods themselves (as may be seen in Fig. 1) passing through holes cast in the cylinder barrel and head. There is also complete enclosure of the overhead rockers (which have return springs no longer fitted), valves and valve springs by means of a very neat rocker-box (cast integral with the cylinder head on O.H.V.s) with quickly-detachable inspection cover giving instant access to the rockers for valve clearance adjustment. On all of the side-valve engines the valves and their springs are also completely enclosed in a valve chest which has a plated detachable cover giving ready access to the adjustable tappets. The valves on all four-stroke engines reciprocate in chilled cast-iron valve guides and are of the finest quality steel with the valve stems hardened by the nitride process. Specially tempered valve springs ensure quick and gas-tight seating of the valves, which are two in number except on some "Bullets" where four are employed (two inlet and two exhaust). Split collet valve spring anchorages are used, except on Model K. An exhaust valve lifter is fitted on the S.V. and

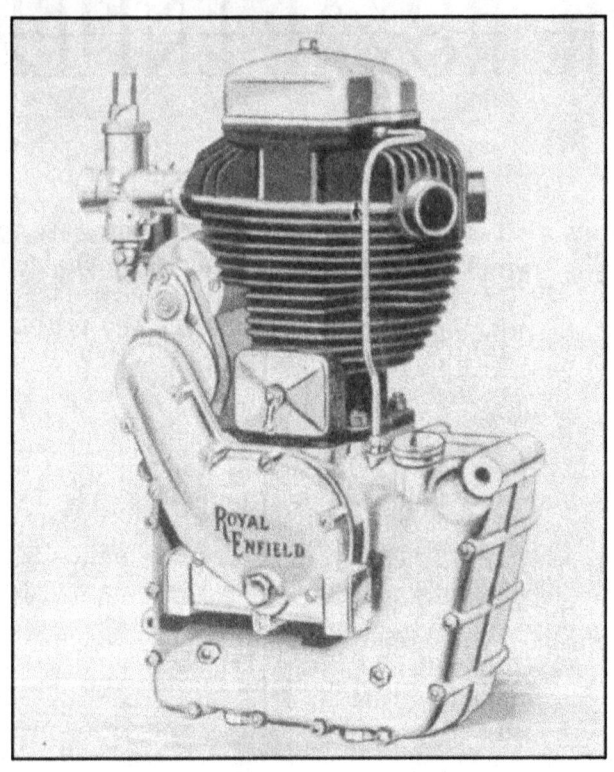

FIG. 1. THE 1938 STANDARD O.H.V. ENGINE
Compactness and cleanliness of design are very apparent. Observe the crankcase oil reservoir, the neat pump housing, the complete valve enclosure, rear "Magdyno" and the feed to the rocker-box

O.H.V. engines (except on Models B, T), but there is no decompressor. All engines are silenced by tubular type silencers.

Lubrication. On the two-stroke models the petroil system of lubrication is employed, in which a quantity of engine oil is mixed in a definite proportion (see page 58) with the fuel in the petrol tank. On the twin-cylinder Model K a dry sump engine lubrication system is included, an Enfield type double-acting plunger oil pump (non-adjustable) drawing oil from the oil compartment of the crankcase and forcing it to the front cylinder and the big-ends, etc., other parts being lubricated by splash. All valves are automatically lubricated.

On the whole of the four-stroke singles a dry sump lubrication system is employed and the system is fully described on page 60. A double-acting plunger type pump worm-driven from the timing side mainshaft draws oil from a finned reservoir or tank cast integral with the crankcase and forces it through an oil feed nozzle projecting into the timing side mainshaft along the

FIG. 2. CLOSE-UP VIEW OF THE S.V. ENGINE
The quick dissipation of heat is ensured by the generous finning provided.

drilled shaft and through the drilled flywheel to the big-end of the connecting-rod. Cylinder lubrication is by splash from the big-end, and surplus oil collecting below the flywheels is returned by the pump to the oil tank. The timing gear is lubricated by oil spray and on all 1938 O.H.V. engines the overhead valves, rocker gear and push-rods are totally enclosed and automatically lubricated. Two large and readily accessible filters ensure that the oil in circulation is kept thoroughly clean, and circulation can be checked by removing the oil reservoir filler cap and noting the return flow of oil.

Carburettor. Amal carburettors are used exclusively. On all models except the lightweights they are of the needle jet type with twist-grip control for the throttle and lever control for the air.

On the lightweights they are of the plain jet type with, in the case of the two-stroke lever, control for both the throttle and air slides. The instruments specified on the overhead-valve models are of the standard Amal type with flange fixing to the inlet port. A slow running adjustment and throttle stop are incorporated to facilitate obtaining A1 tick-over.

Fig. 3. By Merely Undoing Four Nuts the Rear Mudguard can be Instantly Detached

On 350 c.c. and 500 c.c. models the provision of a knock-out spindle and distance piece enables tyre repairs to be effected without removing the wheel.

Ignition. Lodge sparking plugs are fitted as standard, and on all models except Models A, B, T, S, J, H the H.T. current is supplied by a Lucas "Magdyno" which is gear-driven from the inlet camshaft. On the above mentioned models coil ignition is used, the coil being strapped to the saddle pillar and the contact breaker mounted on the end of the Lucas E3E dynamo armature which is gear-driven like the "Magdyno" off the inlet camshaft. Automatic voltage control is standard on all models.

On the coil ignition models a detachable ignition key is incorporated in the centre of the lighting switch which is mounted on the tank panel and a warning lamp is also included. "Magdyno" equipment costs £3 15s. extra.

Frame and Forks. The frame is a duplex type combining exceptional strength and rigidity with a reasonably low weight. It is also designed to provide a really low and comfortable riding position and a ground clearance of 5½ in. Throughout it is constructed of the finest quality weldless steel tubing with liners incorporated where necessary. All except the lightweight models have sidecar lugs incorporated, and on all models it is possible to alter the riding position to suit individual requirements by means of the adjustable rubber mounted handlebars and footrests.

The front forks are of the central compression spring type giving perfect steering and excellent road holding at speed. Tubular fork blades are employed on all but the lightweight models and the 500 c.c. Model J. Shock absorbers are fitted on all models, finger adjustment being provided on the larger models. Steering dampers are also fitted except on the lightweights where they are unnecessary.

Gearbox and Clutch. Enfield four-speed gearboxes of the constant-mesh type with pivotal mounting between the rear engine plates are provided on all except the two-stroke model, which has a three-speed Enfield box. On all except Models A, T, K, KX positive foot change is provided, but on the above models hand control is specified.

The clutch is of the multiple plate type with multi-springs and cork inserts, giving long life and complete absence of fierceness. Control is by a lever on the left of the handlebars operating the clutch by a plunger in the hollow gearbox mainshaft.

Transmission. Coventry roller chains are used for both the primary and secondary transmission. The primary chain on Models C, G, H, J, KX and K is completely enclosed in a cast aluminium oil bath chain case which ensures cleanliness and proper lubrication. On the other models a chain guard is provided for both primary and secondary chains and the former is lubricated by oil mist from an engine breather.

Smoothness of transmission and complete absence of snatch at low speeds in top gear is obtained with the agency of the Royal Enfield patent cush-drive rear hub. This device, besides greatly enhancing riding comfort, also lengthens the life of the entire transmission and the rear tyre. Both driving and rebound shocks are absorbed by blocks of solid rubber enclosed in the rear driving sprocket. The method of construction is clearly shown in Fig. 4. The drum on the driving side of the rear hub has three metal vanes and three similar vanes are incorporated on the inner side of the rear wheel sprocket. Six equal size blocks of solid rubber are inserted between the drum vanes and the wheel sprocket is fitted over the drum so that the sprocket vanes each separate a pair of rubber blocks. Thus there are alternately metal vanes and rubber blocks and their net effect when the engine is running is to damp out all transmission harshness.

Tank. The saddle tank is made of welded steel and is insulated from road shocks by means of rubber supports. The capacity is

FIG. 4. THE CUSH-DRIVE REAR HUB
This vane and rubber block shock absorber is incorporated in the rear hub of all models to smooth out the transmission.

sufficient for long runs to be undertaken without refuelling and there is no separate oil compartment. Finish is in chromium or black enamel with side panels. Large and comfortable rubber knee-grips are provided on all models.

Electric Lighting Equipment. On all models an electric lighting set is fitted as standard, the current for lighting on Models C, G, L, S2, CO, J2, K being generated by a Lucas "Magdyno" (with the dynamo portion detachable), which is gear-driven at engine speed from the inlet camshaft. The current is fed on these models from a 12 amp.-hr. battery mounted on rubber (except Model T) to a Lucas 515668 headlamp with double-filament bulb and handlebar controlled dimming light. The lighting switch together with the ammeter is housed at the back of the headlamp.

The bulb in the rear lamp is mounted on a rubber diaphragm. On the coil ignition Models A, B, T, S, H, J. CO the equipment is similar, except that a Lucas 36 watt E3HB dynamo is used, together with a Lucas 515728 headlamp (type 515728 on models

H. J, CO), a coil on the saddle pillar and a contact-breaker on the dynamo for ignition. An electric horn is included on all models.

Brakes. These are of the internal expanding type with the shoes lined with a special asbestos fabric (Ferodo BJ), giving smooth and powerful braking, longevity and absence of scoring of the drums. Finger adjustment is provided for both front and rear brakes on all models. Brake drums vary from 5 in. to 8 in. in diameter on different models.

Wheels and Tyres. All wheels are substantially built of heavy gauge spokes and have non-adjustable deep-groove journal type hub bearings. The rear hub incorporates a cush drive (see page 6). On the 350 and 500 c.c. models a knock-out spindle is fitted to the rear hub and on withdrawing this a distance piece can be removed, leaving a gap sufficiently big to allow of a tyre tube being changed without detaching the wheel. Dunlop cord tyres are specified and the covers vary in size from 25 in. $\times$ 3·00 in. to 26 in. $\times$ 3·5 in. on the various machines, the heavier models having, of course, more substantial covers.

Mudguards and Carrier. Wide mudguards which are guaranteed to keep road filth where it belongs are used; the front one is deeply valanced with a mud shield at the base. On all models the rear mudguard is quickly detachable (see Fig. 3), to give access to the rear wheel. A carrier is listed as an extra.

Finish. All bright parts are finished in chromium. Other parts such as the frame, mudguards, etc., are finished in best quality black enamel.

Miscellaneous Equipment. A speedometer is not fitted as standard, but an excellent and reliable Smith trip instrument is obtainable as an extra for £2 10s. The author would emphasize that it is now compulsory for all newly registered machines to be fitted with a speedometer.

On all models a comfortable flexible-top saddle, a comprehensive tool kit, a grease gun and a tyre inflator are included in the general specification.

Models for All Tastes. Altogether there are no less than 23 Royal Enfield models listed for 1938, and prices vary from £33 10s. to £77 10s. Two-stroke, side-valve, overhead-valve and competition enthusiasts are all catered for, and there is a machine to suit all tastes and bank balances. The author feels that it would be a waste of valuable space in this handbook to describe the numerous attractive models and he has therefore contented himself with a tabulated summary of the 1938 range. All machines can be bought by gradual payments if desired, and an illustrated catalogue giving full details of the models can be obtained, post free, from the Enfield Cycle Co., Ltd., of Redditch, on request.

SUMMARY OF THE 1938 ROYAL ENFIELDS

Model	c.c.	Bore and stroke (mm.)	Valves	Ignition	Lubrication	Gearbox	Tyres
A . . .	225	64 × 70	T/str.	C	P	3H	3·00–19
B . . .	248	64 × 77	S.V.	C	D.S.	4F	3·00–19
BM . .	248	64 × 77	S.V.	M	D.S.	4F	3·00–19
T . . .	148	56 × 60	O.H.V.	C	D.S.	4H	3·00–19
TM . .	148	56 × 60	O.H.V.	M	D.S.	4F	3·00–19
C De Luxe	346	70 × 90	S.V.	M	D.S.	4F	3·00–19
CO . .	346	70 × 90	O.H.V.	C	D.S.	4F	3 00–19
CM . .	346	70 × 90	O.H.V.	M	D.S.	4F	3·00–19
S . . .	248	64 × 77	O.H.V.	C	D.S.	4F	3·00–19
SM . .	248	64 × 77	O.H.V.	M	D.S.	4F	3·00–19
S2 De Luxe	248	64 × 77	O.H.V.	M	D.S.	4F	3·00–19
G . . .	346	70 × 90	O.H.V.	M	D.S.	4F	3·25–19
250 "Bullet" .	248	64 × 77	O.H.V.	M	D.S.	4F	3·25–19(R)
350 "Bullet" .	346	70 × 90	O.H.V.	M	D.S.	4F	3·25–19(R)
500 "Bullet" J2	499	84 × 90	O H V	M	D.S.	4F	3·50–19(R)
J . . .	499	84 × 90	O.H.V.	C	D.S.	4F	3·25–19
JM . .	499	84 × 90	O.H.V.	M	D.S.	4F	3·25–19
H . . .	570	85½ × 99¼	S.V.	C	D.S.	4F	3·25–19
HM . .	570	85½ × 99¼	S.V.	M	D.S.	4F	3·25–19
L De Luxe .	570	85½ × 99¼	S.V.	M	D.S.	4F	3·50–19(R)
K . . .	1140	1140	S.V.	M	D.S.	4H	4·00–19
KX De Luxe .	1140	1140	S.V.	M	D.S.	4H	4·00–19
500 Comp. .	499	84 × 90	O.H.V.	M	D.S.	4F	4·00–19(R)

CHAPTER II

DRIVING

Driving Licence. Before any one can drive a motor-cycle on the highway he must hold a driving licence. This is obtainable by persons over the age of 16 from the taxation department of the county, county borough, or town council in whose area the person permanently resides, on payment of a fee of 5s. The licence is valid for one year and must be signed. The form for a driving licence is DL1 and a declaration must be made on this form as to physical fitness. If the applicant has never before 1st April, 1934, held a licence he must undergo a driving test, the fee for which is 7s. 6d., and the application form DL26. A machine must be provided for the test and provisional licences to enable riders to learn to drive are obtainable over the counter for 5s. In addition to the driving licence, the machine itself must be licensed and the rider insured against third-party risks. The cost of the machine or registration licences are as follows—

	For a Year £ s. d.	For a Quarter £ s. d.
1. Solo machines not exceeding 224 lb. in weight and registered prior to 1st January, 1933	1 2 6	6 3
2. Solo machines having an engine capacity not exceeding 150 c.c.	12 0	3 4
3. Solo machines exceeding 150 c.c. but not exceeding 250 c.c.	1 2 6	6 3
4. Solo machines exceeding 250 c.c.	2 5 0	12 5
5. Sidecar outfits (additional duty)	15 0	4 2

Licensing a New Machine. On receipt of the tax form RF 1/2 duly filled in, and a "certificate of insurance" or cover note the taxation authorities will issue a registration book, and the licence itself, which must be carried in a waterproof holder in a conspicuous position on the near side of the machine. The registration book must be kept at the owner's place of residence, and must be produced to any police officer who calls for it at any reasonable time. *It should not be carried on the machine.* The registration book should be returned to the issuing council—

1. When any alteration is made to the vehicle.
2. On sale or change of ownership.
3. On change of address.

4. When a sidecar is attached to a solo machine.
5. When the vehicle is broken up, destroyed, or permanently sent out of the United Kingdom.

Taxation licences are issued for periods of three, six, or twelve months by the council by whom the registration book is issued

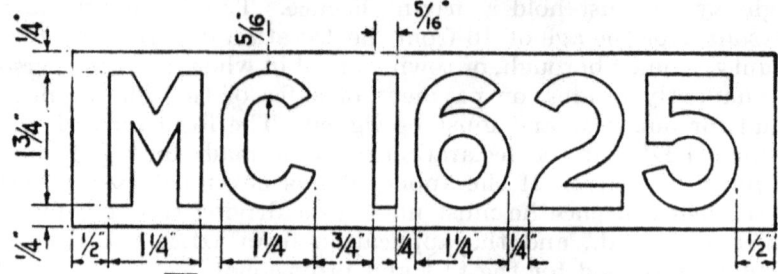

FIG. 5.—FRONT NUMBER PLATE DIMENSIONS

FIG 6.—REAR NUMBER PLATE DIMENSIONS

or by certain chief post offices, subject in the latter case to certain restrictions.

Number Plates. Both in the registration book and on the licence card will be found the index letters and number which have been allotted to the machine, and these must be affixed to the number plates, the lettering being of the dimensions shown in Figs. 5 and 6. One number plate must be effectively illuminated; this is always the rear plate which is shown in Fig. 6.

Horn. An instrument sufficient to give audible warning of the approach of the machine must be fitted and sounded whenever necessary. Neglect to do so may render the driver liable to an action for negligence in the event of an accident. The noise of the machine is insufficient. It is now an offence to sound the horn in "built-up" areas between 11.30 p.m. and 7 a.m.

Brakes. Two brakes, acting independently, must be fitted to the machine, each sufficiently powerful to prevent the wheel on which it takes effect from revolving. Both brakes may be on the same wheel.

Lamps. During the period between one hour after sunset and one hour before dawn (summer time) it is compulsory to show a white light to the front, and a red lamp to the rear. In the case of a sidecar machine, an additional front lamp must be fitted so as to indicate the entire width of the vehicle.

Dangerous Driving. A person driving furiously renders himself liable to a fine of £50, or up to four months' imprisonment for the first offence. He must disclose his name and address to any one who complains that he has driven furiously.

Pillion Riding. No more than one person, in addition to the driver, may be carried on a solo motor-cycle, and such person must sit astride the cycle, and on a proper seat securely fitted behind the driver's seat. He must also be insured.

Duty to Stop. A motor-cyclist must stop his machine, and must remain stationary as long as is reasonably necessary, at the request of any police constable in uniform, or of any person in charge of a horse. A motor-cyclist must also stop if any accident occurs on the highway which is in any way due to the presence of his motor-cycle, whether he be to blame in any way or not.

Driver's Licence. Seventeen is the minimum age for a licence to drive a motor-car, and sixteen for a motor-cycle. No person shall allow another to drive who is not properly licensed.

A declaration of physical fitness must be made at the time of application. The applicant must also declare that he is not disqualified by age or otherwise from obtaining a licence.

On the request of a police officer, the driver shall produce his licence for examination, to enable the officer to ascertain the name and address of the holder of the licence, the date of issue, and the authority by which it was issued. If unable immediately to produce the licence, he cannot be convicted of an offence if, within five days of the request for production, he produces the licence *in person* at any police station he may specify.

Speed Limit. Authority has been given for the general speed limit in built-up areas to be fixed at thirty miles an hour in daylight and 20 m.p.h. during black-out time. A "built-up area" is defined as a length of road in which a system of street lighting is maintained by lamps not more than two hundred yards apart.

Foot Passengers. Foot passengers have a right to walk in the carriage way, which exists equally for them and for vehicles. Drivers must give uninterrupted crossing to persons using recognized pedestrian crossings marked by "Belisha beacons."

Drunkenness. Any person convicted of driving, or attempting to drive, or in charge of a motor vehicle on a road or other public place, when under the influence of drink or drugs to such an extent as to be incapable of having proper control of the vehicle, shall be liable—

(a) On summary conviction, to a fine not exceeding £50 or imprisonment up to four months. For a second or subsequent conviction, to a fine not exceeding £100 or up to four months' imprisonment, or to both such fine and imprisonment.

(b) On conviction on indictment, to imprisonment up to six months, or to a fine (unlimited) or to both imprisonment and fine.

A police-constable may arrest, without warrant, any person committing this offence.

Unless, for special reasons, the Court thinks otherwise, disqualification for a period of twelve months shall follow a conviction. Particulars of conviction and disqualification shall be endorsed on the driving licence.

Obstruction. A motor-cycle must not be left without precautions having been taken against its being started in the absence of the rider. The rider must always stop the engine on leaving it. The machine must not be left on the highway for an unnecessary or unreasonable time, and it must not be left in such a position as to cause obstruction to other users of the highway.

Accidents. A rider who is involved in an accident should at once take steps to ascertain the names and addresses of all those who witnessed the accident, and the name and address of any other party who was involved. A note should be made of the width and condition of the road, and the distances from the point of impact to either kerb. Other points to note are—

1. The speeds of the parties involved.
2. What warning of approach was given.
3. The direction in which the other party was travelling.

DRIVING

4. The manner in which the other party was driving.
5. The width of the road and any other relevant measurements.
6. The tracks of the vehicles concerned, especially noting any signs of the application of brakes.
7. Whether the other vehicle was carrying lamps in accordance with the law. (This applies after dark only.)

It is permissible to point out to a witness any points which are so noted, and it is certainly advisable to do so.

If any person has been injured by the accident, and a claim is likely to be made, it is as well to instruct an independent doctor to report on the injuries. Under the 1930 Road Traffic Act, the accident must be reported within 24 hours at a police station or to a police constable.

Under no circumstances whatever should any admissions be made, nor should any money be offered to any other party, since such payment may seriously prejudice the case. Except under legal advice, no letters should be written. Such advice can be obtained free of charge by members of the Auto-Cycle Union. the Automobile Association, and the Royal Automobile Club.

Road Signs. Certain road signs, which it is incumbent on drivers to observe, are shown in Fig. 9. These signs are placed on the near side of the road.

Interviews with the Police. When stopped for any offence on the road, however ridiculous it may seem, remember that it never pays to be rude to the police. They will always have the opportunity to get their own back in court. At the same time, do not forget that you have a defence to prepare, and that you are entitled to ask any questions you like. If you are stopped for making too much noise, observe whether the constable measures your silencer. If he does not, you may be able to ask awkward questions in court. When the case comes on, if you possibly can, answer the summons in person, as most magistrates dislike absentee defendants, and fine them more heavily than those who attend, quite irrespective of the gravity of the offence.

ON THE ROAD

A novice, with no previous experience of motor-cycling, will find it as well to spend a few minutes in the garage experimenting with the controls, with the engine running in neutral, before taking the machine on the road. When he is well accustomed to the action of the various levers (see Fig. 7), and knows the position of each one, so that he can place his hand on it without taking his eyes off the road, he should preferably take the machine to the top of a gentle slope and coast down it a few times, in order

14   BOOK OF THE ROYAL ENFIELD

to accustom himself to the weight and "feel" of the machine He will find that a motor-cycle, owing to the low disposition of the weight, is a great deal more easy to balance than is an ordinary pedal cycle.

The petrol tap should be turned on, and if the machine has coil ignition, switch on the ignition. Partly close the air lever,

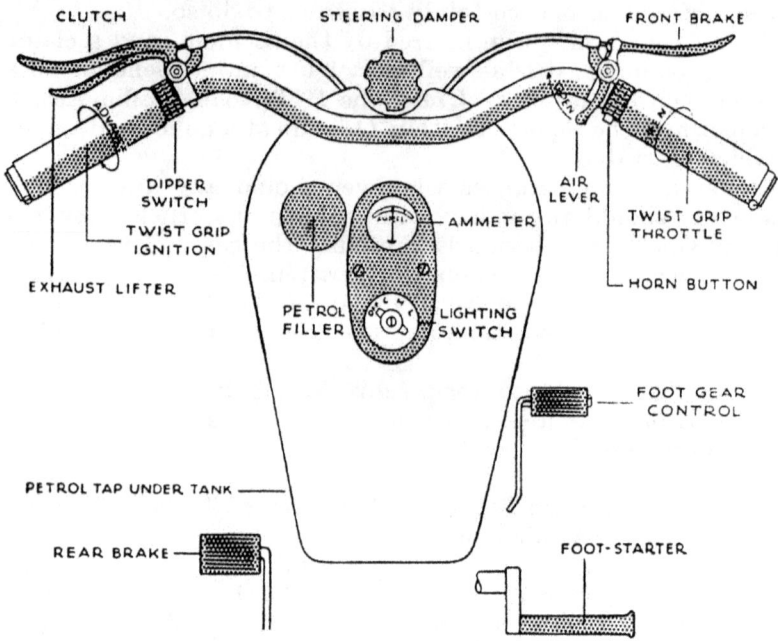

Fig. 7. The 1934–8 Enfield Control Lay-out

Above is shown the lay-out on the O.H.V. models which applies in general to all models. On some single-cylinder S.V. models, however, inverted-type exhaust-valve lifter and front brake levers are used and the rear brake pedal is on the off side. Certain models have an ignition lever (advancing inwards) instead of a twist grip control. On Models B, T and the two-stroke models no exhaust-valve lifter is fitted, inverted clutch and front brake levers being used on the latter. A detachable ignition key is provided in the centre of the lighting switch on coil ignition models. The 1938 models have the ammeter and switch on the headlamp, and since automatic voltage control is provided, there is no switch "C" position.

open the throttle about one-eighth of its travel, and place the spark control about two-thirds advanced. The best positions for the levers for easy starting are found only by experiment, since they vary somewhat for every machine. Thus the overhead valve models start more easily with the spark considerably retarded. Place the gear lever in neutral, and flood the carburettor by depressing the tickler button on the float chamber

DRIVING

lid until petrol runs out. Raise the exhaust lifter (where fitted) and kick the kick-starter hard downwards, releasing the valve lifter when the crank is about half way down. An experienced rider can start the engine in this way with absolute certainty, but it will be found a little tricky until the knack of releasing the valve lifter at the right moment has been acquired.

As soon as the engine fires open the air lever, not too rapidly to its full extent and put the spark lever at full advance.

MOVING OFF

With the engine running in neutral, pull the handlebar clutch-lever right back, and pull the gear lever smartly towards you as far as it will come or press foot lever right up and release. Release the clutch very gently, at the same time opening the throttle somewhat, so that the engine shall not be stopped by putting on to it a load while it is running slowly.

Gear Changing. As soon as the machine is well under way throttle down a little, withdraw the clutch and move the gear-lever forward into the second gear-notch, or press the foot lever right forward and release, and change again into third and fourth gears in a similar manner. You should aim at making gear changes as silently and with as little fuss as possible. Violent acceleration is unnecessary. When in top gear keep air lever wide open and spark fully advanced.

When a hill is encountered, or when it is desired to run more slowly than can be done in top gear, it is necessary to change down. In this case the clutch must be fully withdrawn before the gear-lever is moved. Upward changes should be made as quickly as may be, but, in changing down, one may take one's time, in order that the engine may have time to pick up. A very rapid change down, especially when the engine is running slowly, sometimes pulls the machine up in a harmful manner.

Hill Climbing. The Enfield is capable of surmounting any hills in England and most abroad. It is purely a question of making a fast climb, if this is desired. Hill climbing requires power, and power is only possible with high engine revolutions. *The golden rule, therefore, in hill climbing is to keep the " revs " high* without actually racing the engine. Engine racing, unless the clutch is slipping, is not likely to occur when hill climbing, except on low gear; and the chief concern of the rider is, when driving on the other three gears, to keep the " revs " sufficiently high to enable the power output to be big enough to climb the gradient without changing down. A gear change should, however, be made immediately there is a serious and unavoidable decline in engine revolutions, and a change should be made while the machine still has plenty of momentum. Never carry on on top if this entails letting the " revs " fall away below 1,500 r.p.m., which corresponds to a road speed of about 18 m.p.h., in top gear. *The gear-box is designed for use and should be used.*

When hill climbing, the carburettor controls should be used carefully. Gradually open the throttle as the gradient increases, and very gradually retard the ignition lever or give slightly less air when a slight metallic noise warns the rider that the engine is commencing to labour. Retarding the ignition still further reduces power, so that this action should be delayed until quite necessary. Remember that down-coming traffic is always expected to give way to traffic going up in the event of obstruction being caused. This is a matter of ordinary courtesy.

Descending Hills. There are several methods of doing this, viz. (a) coasting down with the clutch out or gear lever in neutral and the engine off or just ticking-over; (b) descending in gear with the throttle closed, or almost closed.

When descending in gear with the throttle practically closed and the air lever wide open, the engine compression acts as an exceedingly powerful brake, and this braking effect is still greater when the engine revolutions are increased by engaging a lower gear. It is advisable not to entirely close the throttle, owing to the risk of causing a vacuum in the cylinder, which would result in oil being drawn past the rings and fouling the combustion chamber, with consequent plug trouble. After coasting in neutral with engine off (a very pleasant sensation), be careful not to re-engage a gear against full compression. The exhaust valve lifter should be used momentarily and the clutch let in gradually.

Exhaust Lifter. The exhaust lifter is *not* provided for controlling the speed of the machine, which should be done with the throttle, but solely for starting and stopping the engine.

Spark Control. The machine should normally be driven with the spark fully advanced. If, at any time, the engine begins to labour—as, for instance, when picking up after slowing for a corner—the spark should be retarded and advanced again slowly as the engine recovers. Driving under normal circumstances with the spark retarded causes overheating and excessive petrol consumption and damages the exhaust valve.

Brakes. A good driver is sometimes defined as one who drives as though he had no brakes, which may be interpreted to mean that violent acceleration and consequent violent braking are to be avoided. While not everyone will agree with the definition, yet there is no doubt that with the very powerful brakes provided on modern machines, it is easy for an inexperienced rider to provoke a skid which he cannot control. On greasy roads the brakes should be used cautiously, and both front and back should be applied simultaneously, as the machine is then much less liable to skid.

DRIVING A SIDECAR

A rider who has previously driven only solo machines will find

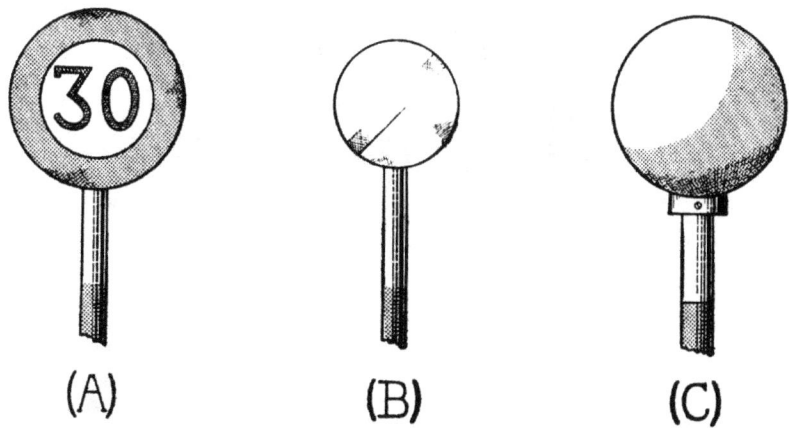

Fig. 8. Three Signs You Must Watch Out For

At *A*, *B*, *C* are shown respectively the 30 m.p.h. speed limit sign indicating a "built-up" area, the derestriction sign which means you can "let her out," and the "Belisha" beacon denoting a pedestrian crossing, where you must give way to persons crossing the road. Another sign to look out for is a triangle within a circle with the words below "HALT AT MAJOR ROAD AHEAD." To disregard this sign is an offence.

that a sidecar outfit feels a little strange at first. Owing to the drag of the sidecar it will seem "hard in the mouth," and difficult to get round a corner. If left-hand corners are taken too fast it will be found that the sidecar wheel leaves the ground, and that the whole outfit tries to turn over. For this reason bends to the left should always be entered slowly, and when the machine is fairly on the corner the throttle may be opened, so that the cycle, accelerating, "runs round" the sidecar. Conversely, on a right-hand corner, the throttle should be partially closed, and it will then be found that the sidecar needs less forcing into the bend.

The beginner will find it surprisingly easy to drive a motor-cycle, for the low centre of gravity and saddle position make the machine much easier to balance than an ordinary bicycle. To ride it well

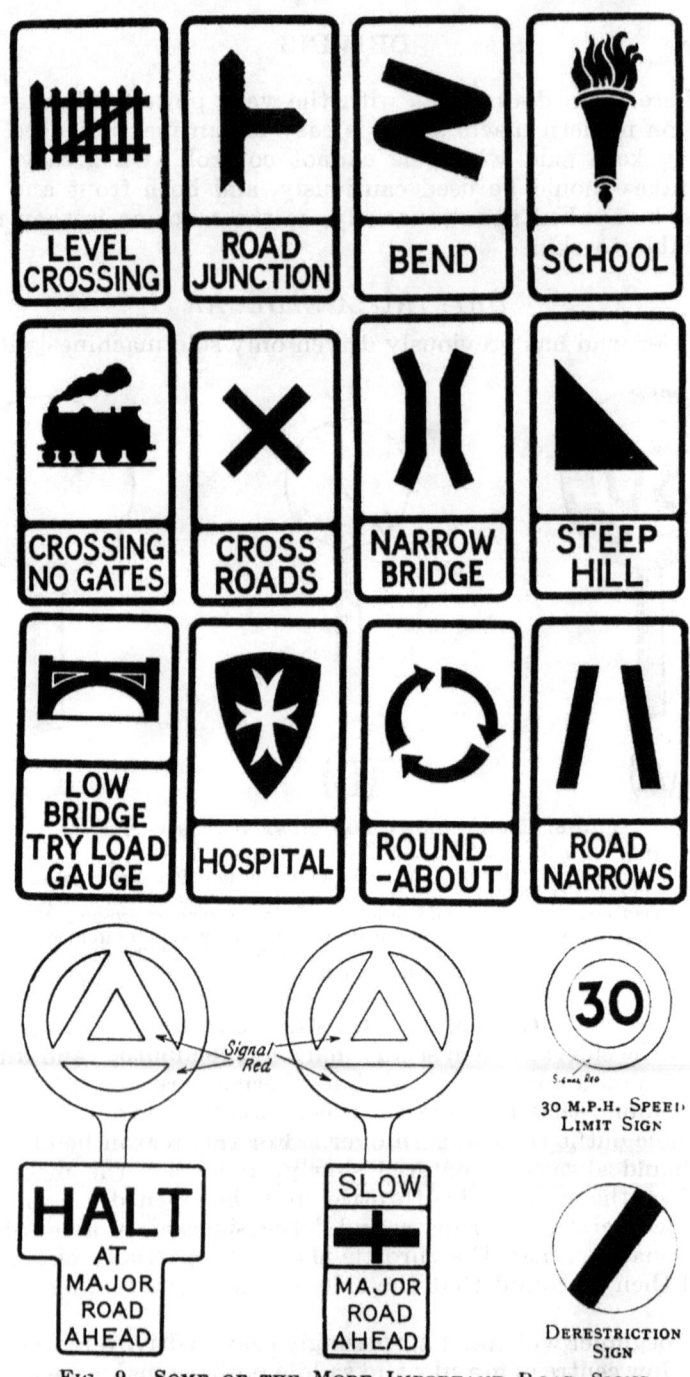

Fig. 9. Some of the More Important Road Signs
(*Reproduced by Courtesy of H.M.S.O.*)

DRIVING

is another matter, but good driving may soon be acquired, for it is indistinguishable from good manners, and the rider who makes it his business to show politeness and courtesy to other users of the road will speedily find his reward in freedom from the minor accidents and narrow shaves which beset the selfish driver. Never, for example, pass a slower vehicle unless the road in front is perfectly clear, and never pass on a corner, for either of these actions may easily force the driver on your left to take refuge in the ditch, should any third vehicle be approaching.

(1) From the front (2) From behind (3) From both directions (4) (5)

FIG. 10.—POLICE SIGNALS FOR STOPPING TRAFFIC COMING FROM THE FRONT, BEHIND, OR FROM BOTH DIRECTIONS

FIG. 11.—SIGNALS FOR RELEASING TRAFFIC

NOTE. Signals Nos. 1 and 5, or 2 and 5, are also used in combination

Despite the opinions of the police and others, speed, as such, is in no way dangerous, provided that it is not indulged in in the wrong place. The danger of the speed merchant is that he sometimes travels fast in unsuitable places, and then finds himself unable to pull up in an emergency.

Never omit to give the recognized hand signals for the benefit of following drivers, and, above all, to give the correct ones. To turn left hold your right arm straight out and then rotate it from the shoulder in an *anti-clockwise* direction.

When turning right extend the right arm and hand, with the palm to the front, and hold them rigid in a horizontal position. If about to stop or slow down, extend the right arm with the palm of the hand turned downwards, and move the arm slowly up and down, keeping the wrist loose. To indicate that you wish to be overtaken, extend the right arm and hand below the level of the shoulder, and move them slowly backwards and forwards.

Beware of Trams. The drivers *never* signal when they are about to turn across the road. In some cities it is forbidden to pass tramcars on the inside, but before passing outside them be sure that no other tram is approaching on the other set of rails. It is unpleasant to be squashed. Do not follow too closely behind a tram. They can stop a great deal more quickly than any other vehicle.

Driving Off the Highway. It should be noted that it is now illegal to *drive* off the public highway on to commons, etc., for more than a distance of 15 yd. for parking purposes. The only exception to this law is in case of an emergency when preventing an offence, extinguishing fire, saving life, etc.

Keep the Brakes Perfect. Every "R.E." owner should frequently give his brakes the "once over." Quite apart from the question of personal safety and the safety of others, it may be mentioned that the police are now empowered to test brakes either on the road or in the garage (subject to the owner's permission).

Smooth Tyres Illegal. It is now illegal to continue to run tyres after the tread has worn away and it may thus be far from economical to extract the last mile from a tyre. In any case smooth tyres invite skidding.

Sign Your Driving Licence. A driving licence must as soon as issued be signed by the owner. Presenting an unsigned licence to the police may incur a "blue paper"!

Speedometer. Every motor cycle other than an invalid carriage or a motor cycle of 100 c.c. or under must be fitted with an instrument to indicate to the driver (within a 10 per cent margin) when the speed limit is being exceeded (see page 12).

If You Fit a Mascot. Be sure not to affix a mascot to the front mudguard in such a position or of such a kind that it is liable to cause injury in the event of a collision with a pedestrian. Neglect in this matter is punishable under a new regulation.

To Purchasers of New Machines. There is one point which the author has not up to now mentioned, and this is of absolutely vital importance.

If you desire to obtain the best results from your Royal Enfield you should not exceed 30 m.p.h. for the first 200 miles, and not until at least 500 miles have been covered should you turn the twist-grip more than half-way open. After doing this mileage it is fairly safe to indulge in a few brief "blinds," but you should not keep the machine running on full throttle *continuously* until after 1000 to 1500 miles have been covered. Quite a number of riders think that after doing 500 miles it is safe to career along the roads all out for miles on end and later on they find that their machines have lost much of their performance and wonder why. Remember prevention is better and cheaper than cure.

DRIVING 21

War-time Lighting Restrictions. If you propose to drive during black-out hours you must have a mask fitted to your head-lamp, and it is advisable to purchase one of the officially approved types. There are a number of these on the market and provided they are not tampered with you should be immune from police attention in this direction.

During foggy weather it is permissible to use the head-lamp *unmasked*, provided (1) the beam is directed downwards towards the near-side; (2) it is used only when fog conditions really demand it; and (3) it is immediately extinguished when an air-raid warning is given. Should a police officer not consider the fog dense enough to warrant the use of the unmasked lamp he has authority to order the light to be extinguished.

The bulb used in the parking and rear lamps must not exceed 7 watts in power and the reflector must be painted black or rendered non-effective. Light may be emitted only through a single aperture facing to the front or rear as the case may be, of not more than 2 in. diameter. Side panels must be completely blacked-out. Also, the aperture through which the light is emitted must be partially obscured by placing behind the glass, paper or some such other uncoloured material having a density equal to that of two sheets of newspaper, or by applying a thin coat of paint to the interior of the glass in such a manner that approximately the same effect is produced. The paper, paint or whatever material is used must cover the whole of the portion of the front glass through which light can pass and must not be treated in any way to increase its transparency.

Stoplights may still be used provided they are so masked that the aperture through which light is emitted is of an area not exceeding 2 sq. in.; the aperture must also be treated in the same way as the side lamps.

CHAPTER III

MECHANICAL FIRST PRINCIPLES

CONSIDERED as a mechanical structure, a motor-cycle consists of three essentials—
1. The cycle frame and wheels, with their fittings, which have been gradually evolved from the equivalents of pedal cycle practice.
2. The engine, which provides the power for driving the machine, with its adjuncts.
3. The means employed for conveying the power of the engine to the back wheel, called the transmission.

The essential parts of an internal combustion engine consist of a cylinder, in which reciprocates a piston, joined by a connecting rod to a crank carried on a crankshaft.

THE FOUR-STROKE ENGINE

Cylinder. The cylinder is composed of cast-iron, closed at the upper, and open at the lower end. Externally, it is surrounded by radiating fins, which are cast on to it for the purpose of dissipating the heat produced by the explosion. Internally, it is ground to a perfectly smooth surface, on which the piston slides.

Piston. The piston, which on modern engines is made of aluminium alloy, has a flat or slightly domed top, and has cut round it, near the top, grooves, in each of which is placed a ring of springy iron. The purpose of these rings, which are called " piston rings," is to press against the cylinder walls, and thus to form a gas-tight joint between the cylinder and the piston. About half-way down, a hole is drilled through the piston skirt from side to side, and in this hole is carried a steel shaft, or pin, called the " gudgeon pin."

Gudgeon Pin. The gudgeon pin serves to connect the piston to the upper or " small " end of the connecting rod, which is formed into a circular eye carrying an anti-friction " bush " or lining of phosphor-bronze, through the centre of which the gudgeon pin passes. Holes drilled through the eye and bush are to admit oil to the gudgeon pin.

Connecting Rod. This is a steel H-section stamping, formed at

MECHANICAL FIRST PRINCIPLES

the lower or " big " end, into an eye similar to that at the small end, but considerably larger.

Crank. The big end of the connecting rod encircles a steel pin called the crank pin, and between the two lie two rows of small steel rollers, forming a roller bearing, which take the heavy load imposed by the combustion of fuel above the piston.

Flywheels. The crank pin is carried between two heavy discs, and is offset from their centre line (see Fig. 13). These discs, or flywheels, are carried inside the aluminium crankcase on which the cylinder is mounted.

Mainshafts. One mainshaft of the flywheels projects through the left side of the crankcase, and carries a toothed sprocket for the driving chain. The other mainshaft has a pinion (" cogwheel " is the term more often applied to the same thing in domestic machinery) which drives the mechanism controlling the valves which admit fuel to the cylinder, and enables the burnt gases to leave it.

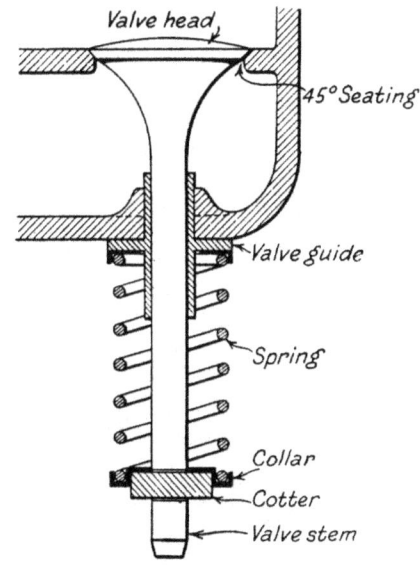

FIG. 12. VALVE WITH SPRING AND COTTER

(A split collet is used on all single-cylinder models, see Fig. 61, instead of a flat cotter.)

Valves. The valves (Fig. 12), which are two in number, or three in the case of LO, LO2, consist of nearly flat circular heads with a long stem having a slot near the end. The under edges of the heads are bevelled at 45°, and rest on the edges of holes in the cylinder, which are similarly bevelled, and thus form a gas-tight joint. The stem of the valve slides in a cast-iron guide, pressed securely into the cylinder casting, and the head is held down on to its seating by a strong spring, which bears or presses at one end on the valve guide, and at the other on a collar round the valve stem. This collar is retained in place by a split collet passing over a recessed taper in the valve stem. (Models K, KX have a flat cotter.)

We are now in a position to describe the working of a four-stroke engine. Fig. 13 represents a greatly simplified engine in section, i.e. cut through vertically. In this engine the exhaust valve is shown on the right, the inlet on the left.

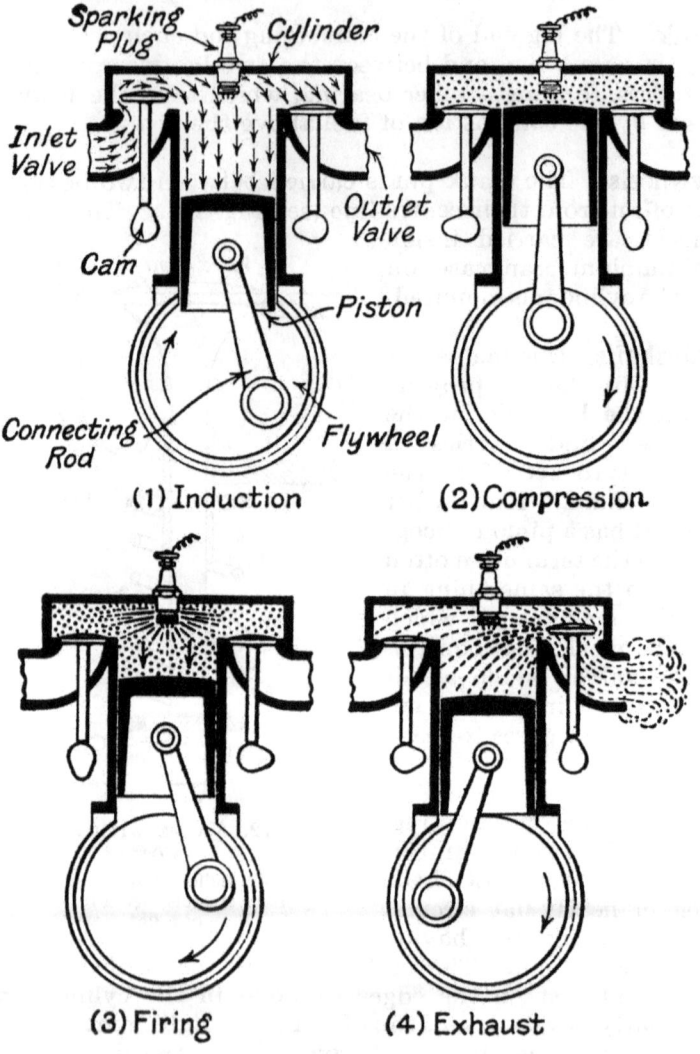

Fig. 13. The Four-stroke Cycle
Note the positions of the piston and valves during each of the four strokes

Consider (1). Here the piston is shown near the top of the stroke, just beginning to descend. As this occurs, the inlet valve is opened (the mechanism will be described later), and the descending piston sucks into the cylinder an explosive mixture of petrol vapour and air. Just beyond the bottom of the stroke, when the piston is beginning to rise, the inlet valve closes, and the mixture is compressed by the rising piston (2). When the piston reaches the top (3), an electric spark passes between the points of the sparking plug in the head of the cylinder, and the mixture is ignited. The force of the explosion drives the

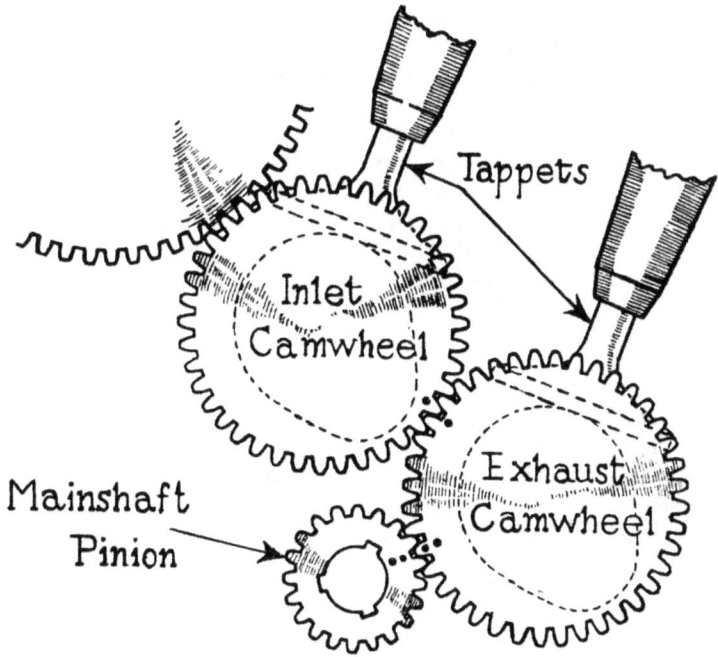

Fig. 14. Simple Timing Gear

piston down, both valves remaining closed until near the bottom of the stroke, when the exhaust valve opens. The momentum of the flywheel carries the piston up to the top again, thus expelling the burnt gases through the open exhaust valve, which closes when the piston reaches the top of the stroke. The inlet valve then opens again, and the cycle is repeated.

It will be seen that there are four strokes of the piston to each explosion, hence the term " four-stroke."

Timing Gear. The timing gear, or mechanism which controls the opening of the valves and the passage, at the correct moment, of the spark, is simpler than many novices imagine.

The pinion on the right-hand end of the mainshaft (see Fig. 14) meshes with two other wheels which, having twice as many teeth, turn at half the speed of the mainshaft pinion. These large wheels (called the "camwheels") carry two cams, which are simply steel discs of irregular, as opposed to circular, shape. The shape, which rather resembles that of a pear, is shown in Fig. 14.

Tappets. The tappets are simply small steel rods, working in guides pressed into the upper face of the timing gear case, and having at their upper (outside) ends an adjustment for length. The upper end of the tappet is immediately below the lower end of the stem of its valve on side-valve engines.

It will be perceived that when the cam is turned, as soon as the raised part comes under the flat base tappet, the latter will raise the valve. Since the cams rotate once only to every two revolutions on the mainshaft, each valve opens once only in two crankshaft revolutions, i.e. in four strokes of the piston. The correct moment at which the valves open and close is arranged for by the correct meshing of the mainshaft pinion and the camwheel. The teeth in each pinion which mesh together are usually marked with punch marks (see Fig. 14).

Push-rods. On overhead-valve engines where the valve stems point upwards instead of downwards as on the side-valve engines, tubular steel rods known as "push-rods" are placed between the tappets and overhead rockers which actuate the valves. The cam raises the tappet, this raises the push-rod, and the upper end of the rod moves the rocker, which in turn pushes down the valve.

Exhaust Lifter. Incorporated also except on Models B, T is a device, controlled by Bowden cable from the handlebar, for raising the exhaust valve a short distance off its seating, irrespective of the position of the cam. The purpose of the exhaust lifter is, by releasing the compression, to make it easier to start and stop the engine.

Magneto Drive. The end of the camshaft on the twin-cylinder model is extended through a bearing in the timing case cover, and carries on its tapered end a sprocket wheel. Over this sprocket runs a chain, which drives another sprocket on the magneto shaft, of the same size as the camshaft sprocket. The magneto thus runs at half-engine speed. On the single cylinder Royal Enfield models the magneto is driven by two gears from the inlet cam wheel (see Fig. 54) and rotates at half-engine speed. The working of the magneto and coil ignition used on some models is described on pages 41 and 43.

In addition to a range of four-stroke models, the Enfield Cycle Co., Ltd., also manufacture one lightweight two-stroke machine.

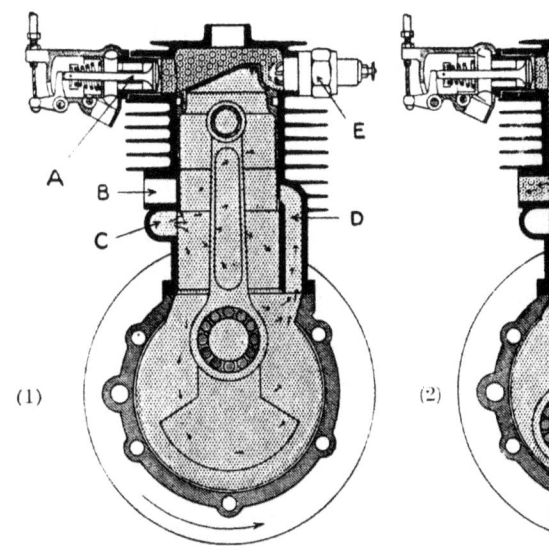

(1) A—Compression release valve. B—Exhaust port. C—Inlet port. D—Transfer port. E—Sparking plug. Compressed gas just being fired. Fresh charge of gas entering crankcase.

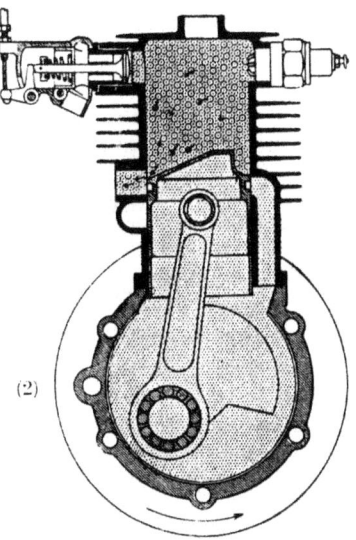

(2) Piston on downward stroke—uncovering exhaust port in its descent. Exhaust gases commencing to pass out. Gas in crankcase compressed.

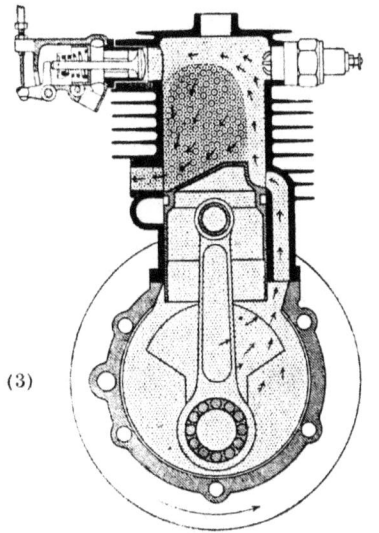

(3) Piston at bottom of stroke. Exhaust and transfer ports open—inlet port closed. Fresh charge passing into cylinder. Exhaust gases passing out, shaded dark.

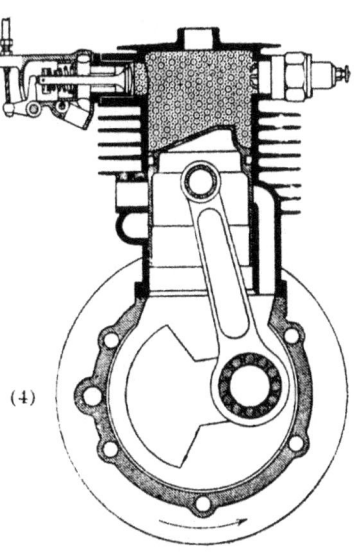

(4) Piston rising on upward stroke. Gas being compressed in cylinder—partial vacuum being formed in crankcase. All ports closed.

FIG. 15.—PRINCIPLE OF TWO-STROKE ENGINE

On the small Royal Enfield engines a compression release valve is not fitted.

THE TWO-STROKE ENGINE

The two-stroke engine, as its name implies, fires once for every two strokes of the piston, or at every revolution of the crankshaft. It is, moreover, a somewhat simpler type than the four-stroke, since there are no valves or timing gear.

The cylinder head is perfectly plain, having in it an aperture only for the sparking plug, for no compression release valve is fitted on Royal Enfield two-stroke engines.

(*From "The Motor Cycle"*)

Fig. 16. The 225 c.c. Royal Enfield Two-stroke Engine

The above sketch shows the power unit fitted on Model A. The flange fitting two-lever, non-needle Amal carburettor and the chain-driven dynamo with contact breaker on the flywheel side for coil ignition are clearly shown.

About half-way down the cylinder wall three holes, or "ports," are cut. Of these the lowest, the inlet port, has outside it a short pipe, to the end of which the carburettor is bolted. Just above the inlet port, and slightly to one side, is the exhaust port, and opposite this is the transfer port, which communicates, by the transfer passage, which is cast into the cylinder wall, with the crankcase. Precautions are taken to render the crankcase airtight, and the flywheel is carried outside it on the right side.

The action is as follows. The length of the piston is so arranged that, when it reaches the top of the stroke, the inlet port, but not the transfer or exhaust ports, shall be entirely below it. The fuel mixture from the carburettor has thus a clear passage

MECHANICAL FIRST PRINCIPLES

into the crankcase. When the piston rises, it leaves a partial vacuum in the airtight crankcase, into which fuel mixture flows as soon as the inlet port is uncovered by the piston skirt. The piston then descends, compressing the mixture beneath it in the crankcase. When near the bottom of the stroke, the transfer and exhaust ports are uncovered by the *top* of the piston. The compressed charge in the crankcase, therefore, flows through the transfer passage into the cylinder, where it is directed upwards by the peculiarly-shaped deflector top of the piston. At the same time, the burnt gases of the previous charge find their way out of the exhaust port on the opposite side of the cylinder. The piston rises again, closing the exhaust and transfer ports, and compresses the charge, which is fired at the top of the stroke by an electric spark, just as in the case of the four-stroke engine. While this compression stroke is taking place on one side of the piston, a fresh charge of petrol and air is being sucked into the crankcase on the other, the two motions taking place simultaneously.

Since the two-stroke engine fires twice as often as the four-stroke, the magneto is driven twice as fast, i.e. at engine speed. On the Royal Enfield two-strokes, it is driven by chain from a sprocket mounted on the engine shaft between the driving sprocket and the crankcase.

Cubic Capacity. It will be appreciated that the greater the volume of that part of the cylinder through which the piston moves (the " swept volume ") the greater will be the amount of gas drawn into the cylinder and exploded when the engine fires ; and hence the greater will be the power developed by the engine. The " cubic capacity " of the cylinder is therefore a measure of the power of the engine. This capacity is measured in cubic centimetres, commonly abbreviated into "c.c." For taxation purposes 100 c.c. is equal to 1 h.p. Thus Model K, which has a capacity of 1140 c.c., is rated at 11·4 h.p.

Principle of the Gear-box. It will be evident that, if two pinions of unequal size are meshed together, the circumferences of both wheels must run at the same speed, and that the smaller must rotate at a higher number of revolutions per minute than the larger. A gear-box has, therefore, to contain two shafts on which the pinions are mounted. Instead, however, of driving one shaft, and taking the drive to the back wheel from the other, it is found that a smaller and more efficient box can be made by making the reduction of gear in two steps. A large pinion on one shaft drives a smaller one on a second shaft. This small pinion drives a large one on the same shaft, which drives the other end of the first shaft through a fourth (small) pinion. In this way all the pinions can be made smaller, and it is also possible to arrange for a direct drive on top gear, when the power does not pass

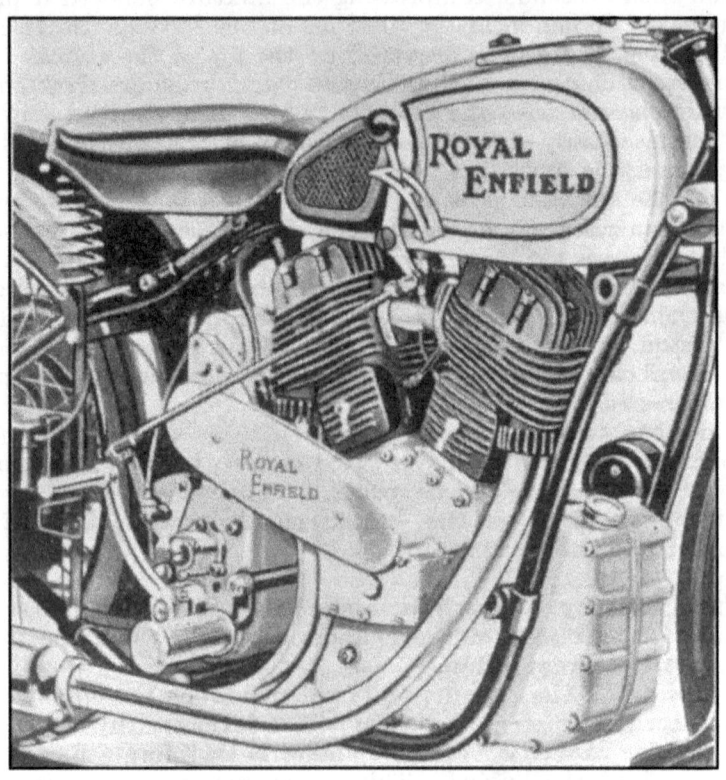

FIG. 17. THE 1938 1140 C.C. TWIN-CYLINDER S.V. ENGINE
This engine, a cut-away view of which is shown in Fig. 33, is fitted to the magnificent Big Twins, Models K, KX.

through any of the pinions. The shaft in a gear-box which takes the drive from the engine, and from which the power is transmitted to the back wheel, is called the "mainshaft," and the other shaft is called the "layshaft."

CHAPTER IV

THE CARBURETTOR AND IGNITION

The Principle of the Carburettor. It has been found by experiment that the most satisfactory way of encouraging petrol to evaporate is to drive it under pressure through a very tiny hole, called a jet, and the process is assisted by heating the spraying

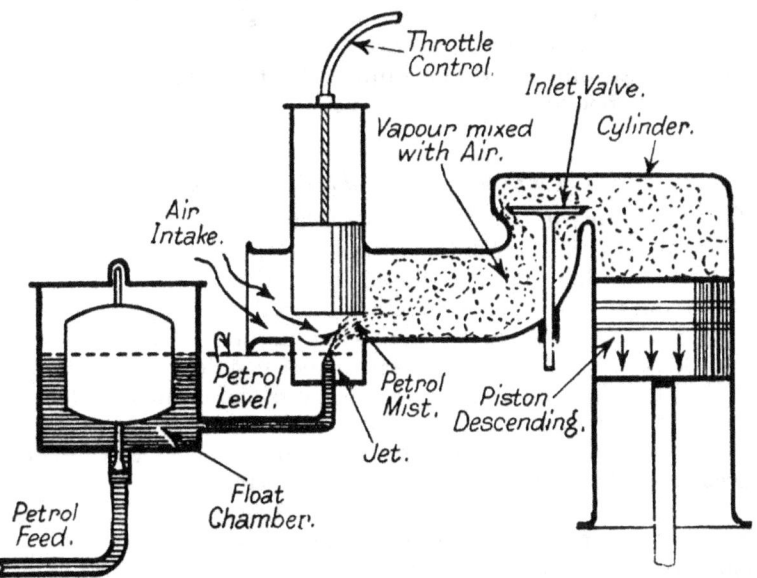

FIG. 18. THE PRINCIPLE OF THE CARBURETTOR

device. Owing to the proximity of the carburettor to the combustion chamber, ample heat is, of course, conducted to it *via* the induction pipe, once the engine has warmed up. The powerful suction through the inlet pipe on the inlet stroke can be relied upon to atomize the fuel completely. Let us refer to Fig. 18, which shows the salient features of a carburettor in action. It will be observed that the petrol level in the jet must be below the orifice at the top, otherwise the petrol will overflow and cause *flooding* of the carburettor. The level is automatically regulated by the action of a *float* attached to a spindle, which operates a needle valve, thereby cutting off the petrol supply immediately the level in the chamber reaches the height of the jet orifice.

On the downward stroke of the piston, air is sucked in through the air-intake; past the partially open throttle, which is a closely-fitting hand-controlled slide, operating up and down in a barrel; past the jet; past the inlet valve, and thence into the cylinder. The extremely high velocity air current that must obviously sweep over the jet causes the fuel to issue in a small fountain, and simultaneously causes the spirit to be atomized and diffused with the air rushing in towards the combustion chamber. This, briefly, is the principle of the carburettor.

The various refinements and complications that are incorporated in the Amal carburettor are designed to (1) make the mixture as homogeneous as possible; (2) simplify the control; (3) enable automatic slow running to be obtained; (4) enable settings for special purposes to be made.

THE AMAL-NEEDLE JET CARBURETTOR

This carburettor is fitted on all 1934-8 Models except Models A, T, and the 1935-6 Model B, and the following description will enable the reader to comprehend its working.

Referring to Fig. 19, showing a sectional view of the instrument, A is the carburettor body or mixing chamber, the upper part of which has a throttle valve B, with taper needle C attached by the needle clip. The throttle valve regulates the quantity of mixture supplied to the engine. Passing through the throttle valve is the air valve D, independently operated, and serving the purpose of obstructing the main air passage for starting and mixture regulation. Fixed to the underside of the mixing chamber by the union nut E is the jet block F, and interposed between them is a fibre washer to ensure a petrol-tight joint. On the upper part of the jet block is the adaptor body H, forming a clear through-way. Integral with the jet block is the pilot jet J, supplied through the passage K. The adjustable pilot air-intake L communicates with a chamber, from which issues the pilot outlet M and the by-pass N. An adjusting screw (TS, Fig. 20) is provided on the mixing chamber, by which the position of the throttle valve for tick-over is regulated independently of the cable adjustment. The needle jet O is screwed in the underside of the jet block, and carries at its bottom end the main jet P. Both these jets are removable when the jet plug Q, which bolts the mixing chamber and the float chamber together, is removed. The float chamber, which has bottom feed, consists of a cup R suitably mounted on a platform S containing a float T, and the needle valve U attached by the clip V. The float chamber cover has a lock-screw X for security.

The petrol tap having been turned on, petrol will flow past the needle valve U until the quantity of petrol in the chamber R

THE CARBURETTOR AND IGNITION

is sufficient to raise the float T, when the needle valve U will prevent a further supply entering the float chamber until some in the chamber has already been used up by the engine. The

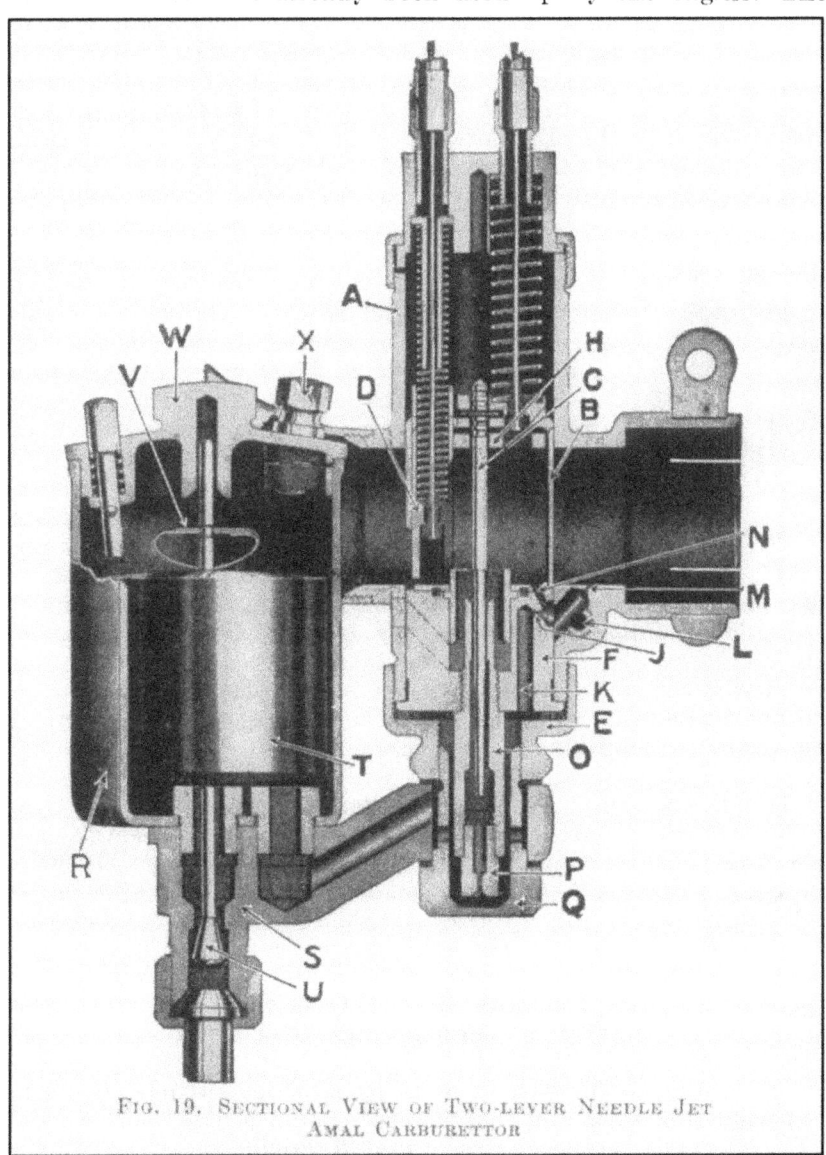

Fig. 19. Sectional View of Two-lever Needle Jet Amal Carburettor

float chamber having been filled to its correct level, the fuel passes along the passages through diagonal holes in the jet plug Q, when it will be in communication with the main jet P and the pilot feed hole K; the level in these jets being, obviously, the same as that maintained in the float chamber.

Imagine the throttle valve B very slightly open. As the piston descends, a partial vacuum is created in the carburettor, causing a rush of air through the pilot air hole L, and drawing fuel from the pilot jet J. The mixture of air and fuel is admitted to the engine through the pilot outlet M. The quantity of mixture capable of being passed by the pilot outlet M is insufficient to run the engine. This mixture also carries excess of fuel. Consequently, before a combustible mixture is admitted, throttle valve B must be slightly raised, admitting a further supply of air from the main air-intake. The farther the throttle valve is opened, the less will be the depression on the outlet M, but, in turn, a higher depression will be created on the by-pass N, and the pilot mixture will flow from this passage as well as from the outlet M. As the throttle valve is farther opened the fuel passes the main jet P, and this jet governs the mixture strength from seven-eighths to full throttle. For intermediate throttle positions, the taper needle C working in the needle jet O is the governing factor. The farther the throttle valve is lifted, the greater the quantity of air admitted to the engine, and a suitable graduation of fuel supply is maintained by means of the taper needle. The air valve D, which is cable-operated on the two-lever carburettor, has the effect of obstructing the main through-way, and, in consequence, increasing the depression on the main jet, enriching the mixture.

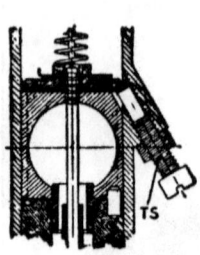

Fig. 20. Amal Throttle Stop

Tuning the Amal Needle Jet Carburettor. Should the setting not give entire satisfaction for particular requirements, there are four separate ways of rectifying matters as given herewith, and the adjustment should be made in this order: (*a*) Main jet (three-quarters to full throttle); (*b*) Pilot air adjustment (closed to one-eighth throttle); (*c*) Throttle valve cut-away on the air-intake side (one-eighth to one-quarter throttle); (*d*) Needle position (one-quarter to three-quarters throttle). The diagram (Fig. 21) clearly indicates the part of the throttle range over which each adjustment is effective.

(*a*) To obtain the correct main jet size, several jets should be experimented with, and that selected should be the *smallest which gives maximum power and speed on full throttle.*

(*b*) To weaken slow running mixture, screw pilot air adjuster outwards, and to enrich screw pilot air adjuster inwards.

Screw pilot air adjuster home in a clockwise direction. Place

THE CARBURETTOR AND IGNITION 35

gear lever in "neutral." Slightly flood the float chamber by gently depressing the tickler until fuel begins to escape from the mixing chamber. Set magneto at half advance, throttle approximately one-eighth open, close the air lever, start the engine, and warm up. After warming up, reduce the engine revolutions by gently throttling down. The slow-running mixture will prove over-rich unless air leaks exist. Very gradually unscrew the pilot jet

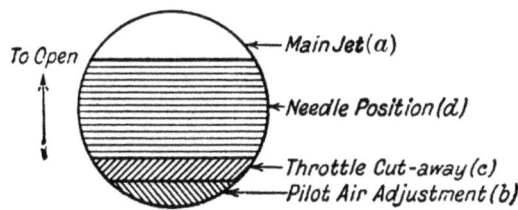

FIG. 21. RANGE AND SEQUENCE OF ADJUSTMENTS—AMAL NEEDLE JET CARBURETTOR

adjuster. The engine speed will increase, and must again be reduced by gently closing the throttle until, by a combination of throttle position and air adjustment, the desired "idling" is obtained. It is occasionally necessary to retard completely the magneto before getting a satisfactory tick-over, especially when early ignition timing is used. If it is desired to make the engine idle with the throttle quite closed, the position of the throttle valve must be set by means of the throttle stop-screw, the twist-grip during this adjustment being turned right home. Alternatively, if the screw is adjusted clear of the throttle valve, the engine will be shut off in the normal way by the twist-grip.

(c) Given satisfactory "tick-over," set the magneto control at half-advance with the air lever fully open. Very slowly open the throttle valve when, if the engine responds regularly up to one-quarter throttle, the valve cut-away is correct.

A weak mixture is indicated by spitting back through the air-intake with blue flames and hesitation in picking up, which disappears when the air lever is closed down. This can be remedied by fitting a throttle valve with less cut-away. A rich mixture is shown by a black, sooty exhaust, and the engine falters when the air valve is closed. The remedy for this is a throttle valve with greater cut-away. Each Amal valve is stamped with two numbers, the first indicating the type number of the carburettor, and the second figure the amount of cut-away on the intake side of the valve in sixteenths of an inch, e.g. 6/4 is a type 6 valve with four-sixteenths, i.e. a $\frac{1}{4}$ in. cut-away.

(d) Open air lever fully and the throttle half-way. Note if the exhaust is crisp and the engine flexible. Close the air valve slightly below the throttle, when the exhaust note and engine revolutions should remain constant. Should popping back and spitting occur with blue flames from the intake, the mixture is weak, and the needle should be slightly raised. Test by lowering the air valve gently. The engine revolutions will rise when the air valve is lowered slightly below the throttle valve.

If the engine speed does not increase progressively with raising of the throttle, and a smoky exhaust is apparent with heavy laboured running, and tendency to eight-stroke, the mixture is too rich and the needle should be lowered in the throttle valve. Having found the correct needle position, the carburettor setting is now complete, and it will be found that the driving is practically automatic once the engine is warmed up. For speed work the main jet may be increased by 10 per cent, when the air lever should be fully open on full throttle.

Maintenance of the Amal Needle Jet Carburettor. Periodical cleaning is necessary to maintain efficient functioning of the carburettor, and should be carried out in the following sequence—

Disconnect petrol pipe. Unscrew holding bolt Q (Fig. 19) and remove float chamber complete. With box or set spanner, slacken the mixing chamber union nut E. Mixing chamber complete may now be removed from engine, either by unscrewing the clip pin (if outlet) or the bolts (if flange fitting). Unscrew mixing chamber lock ring, and pull out throttle valve needle and air valve. Remove main jet P and needle jet O. Mixing chamber union nut E may then be removed and jet block complete pushed out. If this is obstinate, tap gently, using a wooden stump inside the mixing chamber. Unscrew float chamber cover W and slacken lock screw X. Withdraw the float by pinching the clip V inwards, and at the same time pull gently upwards.

Generally it is sufficient to wash all the parts in clean petrol, but if the carburettor has had extended service, check the following—

(*a*) FLOAT CHAMBER NEEDLE U. If a distinct shoulder is visible on the point of seating, renew this as soon as convenient.

(*b*) THROTTLE VALVE. Test in mixing chamber, and if excessive play is present it is advisable to renew this without delay.

(*c*) THROTTLE NEEDLE CLIP. This part must securely grip needle. *Free rotation must not take place,* otherwise the needle groove will become worn and necessitate a new part being fitted. *Be sure to refit the clip in the same groove.*

(*d*) JET BLOCK. If trouble has been experienced with erratic "idling," ascertain by means of a fine bristle that the pilot jet J is clear, and that the pilot outlet M in the mixing chamber is unobstructed.

THE CARBURETTOR AND IGNITION 37

To Reassemble. Refit jet block *F* with washer on underside, and screw on lightly mixing chamber union nut *E*. Screw in needle jet *O* and main jet *P*. Open air lever $\frac{7}{8}$ in., the twist-grip half-way; grasp the air slide between the thumb and the finger; *make sure that the needle enters the central hole in the adaptor top.* Slightly twist the throttle valve until it enters the adaptor guide,

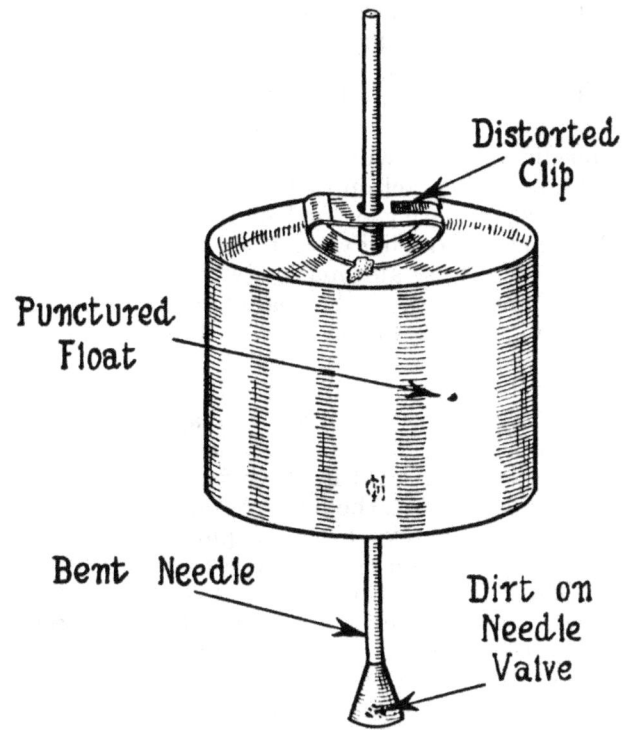

FIG. 22. SOME POSSIBLE CAUSES OF CARBURETTOR FLOODING

when on pushing down the valves the air valve should enter its guide. If not, slightly move the mixing chamber top, when the air valve will slide into place. Screw on mixing chamber lock-nut.

Attach carburettor to the cylinder, pushing right home, and examine washer if flange fitting. Insert holding bolt *Q*, and thoroughly tighten union nut *E* by means of a fixed spanner. Refit float and needle, holding the needle head against its seating by means of a pencil until the float and the clip *V* are slipped into position. Make sure that the clip enters the groove provided. Screw on the cover tightly and lock in position by means of the lock screw *X*. Fit holding bolt in float chamber with one washer above and one below the lug. Screw holding bolt into mixing chamber and lock securely. Clean petrol pipe and filter if fitted.

THE AMAL NON-NEEDLE CARBURETTOR

This carburettor is fitted on 1934–8 Models A, T and the 1935–6 Model B, the 1934–6 Model Z. The following description in conjunction with the sectional view shown in Fig. 22A should enable the reader to understand exactly how it functions.

Referring to Fig. 22A, the petrol tap having been turned on, petrol will flow past the needle valve P until the quantity of petrol in the float chamber G is sufficient to raise the float O, when the needle valve P will prevent a further supply entering the float chamber. The action of the float can readily be understood, for, as the quantity of fuel in the float chamber is used, the float O will drop, carrying with it the needle P, and admitting a further supply. Thus, automatically, the petrol level is kept constant. In connection with the float chamber, it must be clearly understood that any alteration to the standard level can only have detrimental results.

The float chamber having filled to its correct level, the fuel passes along the passages through the diagonal holes in the jet plug H, when it will be in communication with the main jet D and the pilot jet C, the level in these jets being, obviously, the same as that maintained in the float chamber.

Imagine the throttle valve K very slightly open. As the piston descends, a partial vacuum is created in the carburettor, causing a rush of air through the through-way A, and drawing fuel from the pilot jet C. The pilot jet, being situated immediately beneath the base of the throttle valve, is subjected to a heavy depression, so as to obtain the necessary mixture for "idling" and small loads.

In the case of the main jet D, which is the longer of the two, and situated near the carburettor air intake, at small throttle openings it is inoperative, and the mixture is governed entirely by the size of the pilot jet.

The throttle K being almost closed, it will be seen that the pilot jet C is situated in an extremely restricted area. In consequence, the passage of the air from the main through-way will be restricted, and at the same time a high depression will exist on the pilot C. At this position of the throttle, it will readily be seen that not only is the main jet D shrouded by the throttle valve, but also the area of the mixing chamber in which it is housed is infinitely bigger than the area of the through-way exposed to the suction of the engine, in consequence of which no fuel is drawn from the main jet.

As the throttle valve K is raised, the area immediately above the pilot jet *C* is increased, and in consequence the suction or depression on this jet diminishes, and at the same time increases on the main jet, so a balance between the two jets is obtained throughout the whole range.

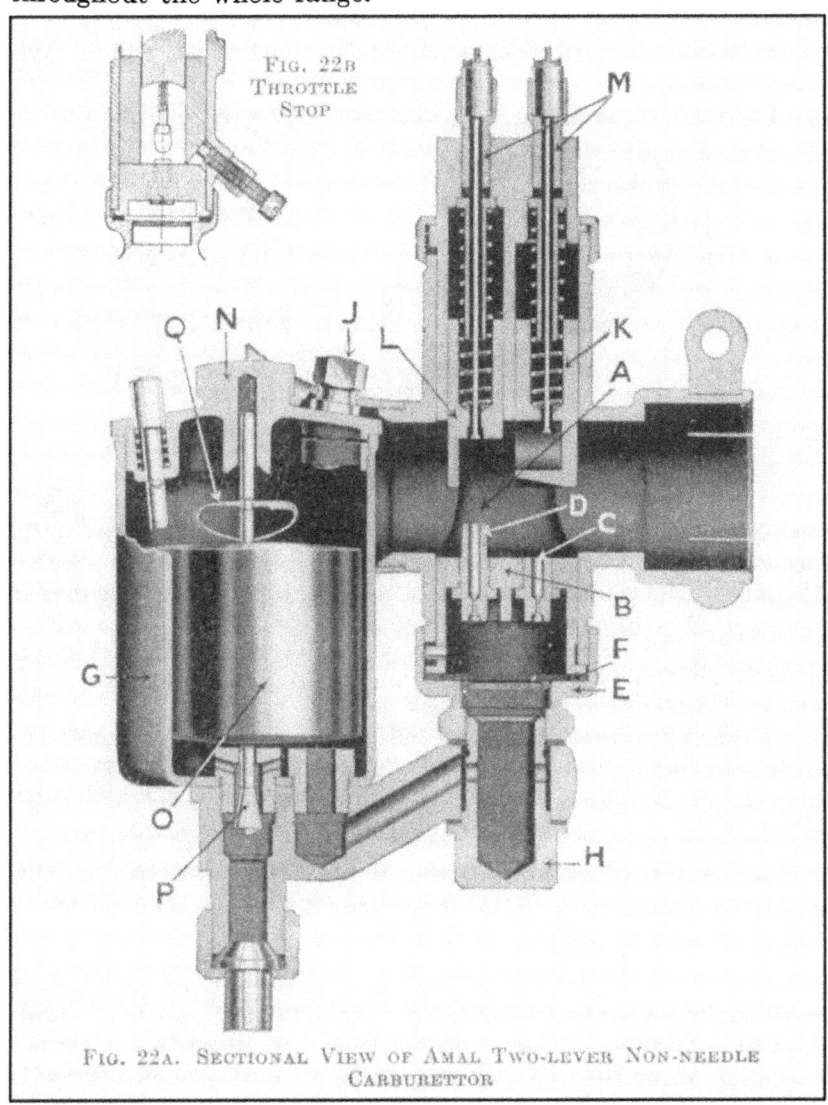

Fig. 22A. Sectional View of Amal Two-lever Non-needle Carburettor.

Tuning Non-needle Carburettor. There are three ways in which the quality of the mixture can be varied, and these are given hereunder in the order in which the adjustments should be made.

(*a*) Main jet (affects the mixture from $\frac{5}{8}$ to full throttle).

(b) Pilot jet (affects the mixture from closed to ¼ throttle).
(c) Throttle valve cut-away (affects mixture from ¼ to ⅜ throttle).

The diagram shown in Fig. 23 clearly indicates the part of the throttle range over which each adjustment is effective.

(a) *Main Jet.* Fit the smallest size main jet which gives

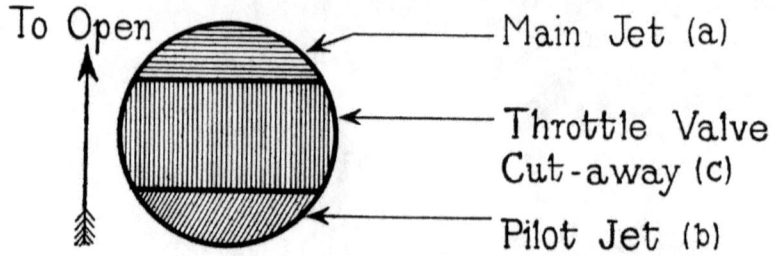

FIG. 23. RANGE AND SEQUENCE OF ADJUSTMENTS—AMAL NON-NEEDLE CARBURETTOR

maximum speed. For touring conditions I advise this to be obtained with the air lever three-quarter open.

(b) *Pilot Jet.* This affects "slow running" and slow pulling only, and the smallest size should be selected which gives the best "idling." At the same time, care must be taken not to reduce the size of the pilot jet unduly, otherwise difficulty will be experienced in obtaining a correct blend with the main jet.

Blend of Main and Pilot. If any trouble is experienced due to a weak spot between the pilot and main jet, it can usually be cured by increasing the pilot jet one size.

(c) *Throttle Valve Cut-away.* Richness at ⅜ to ⅝ throttle can be rectified by fitting a "cut-away" throttle valve. The standard cut-aways are from O, which is flat bottom, to No. 5, which is cut away $\tfrac{5}{16}$ in.

Starting Up. With a *cold engine*, depress the carburettor tickler, close air valve, open throttle about one-eighth, ignition about three-quarter advanced, when, if the ignition system is in good order, no difficulty should be experienced in obtaining an "easy start." With a *warm engine* it is unnecessary to flood carburettor, but the air lever should be closed. If the float chamber is unduly flooded, excessive richness of mixture will prevent the engine starting. Open throttle fully and revolve the engine smartly until excess of fuel is exhausted; then proceed as before, without again flooding.

Maintenance of Amal Non-needle Carburettor. To keep the carburettor in thoroughly efficient working order it is important

THE CARBURETTOR AND IGNITION

to clean it occasionally, as various impurities find their way into the instrument. The best method of cleaning the carburettor and one which the author always adopts is to strip it right down and clean the various parts in petrol. Should any parts appear worn they should be renewed at once, otherwise it is foolish to expect perfect carburation. For instance, renew the needle valve of the float chamber if a distinct ridge is present on the head where it seats; similarly replace the throttle valve if much side play is present; again fit a new mixing chamber union nut if there is any suspicion of this being in any way worn or damaged. Before reassembling clean the filter situated beneath the jets and when reassembling avoid using any brute force to tighten any nuts. Ascertain that the needle enters the top of the float chamber lid easily, that the mixing chamber is quite vertical and pushed tight home, that the washer on flange fitting instruments is in sound condition and that the jets are properly fitted.

When Ordering Spares. Always quote the number which is stamped on the side of the mixing chamber. This will ensure the correct part being sent and will obviate much bother on both the part of the rider and the manufacturer.

THE PRINCIPLE OF THE MAGNETO

The magneto or magneto portion of the "Magdyno" primarily consists of three parts: (1) the *armature*; (2) a *U-shaped magnet*; (3) the *contact breaker*.

The armature comprises an iron core or bobbin of "H" section, on which are two windings; firstly, a short winding of fairly heavy gauge wire; and, secondly, on top of the former, a very big winding of fine wire. The first winding is known as the *primary*, and the second as the *secondary*. (See Fig. 24.) The armature, which can rotate on ball bearings, is placed such that on rotation it periodically cuts across the *magnetic field* of the magnet, and creates a current in the primary winding. Incidentally, the contact breaker forms part of the primary circuit. This current, however, is at a very low voltage—far and away too small to produce anything in the nature of a spark. But if a *break* is suddenly caused in the primary by separating the platinum contacts when the current is at its maximum flow, a high voltage or tension current will be instantly *induced* in the secondary winding—sufficient to jump a small space, if the circuit be incomplete. In this circuit the sparking plug is included, and things are so arranged that, in order for the secondary circuit to be complete, the current must jump across the electrodes of the plug, or, in other words, a spark must occur. Now in the case of a single-cylinder engine, the points in the rotating contact breaker separate once in every armature revolution (there being one cam only), and the armature to which the contact breaker is fitted being driven off the inlet camshaft by a pair of gear wheels runs at half-engine speed; that is to say, a "break" takes place once every two engine revolutions, i.e. four strokes of the piston. Hence if the initial "break" be timed to occur when the piston is at the

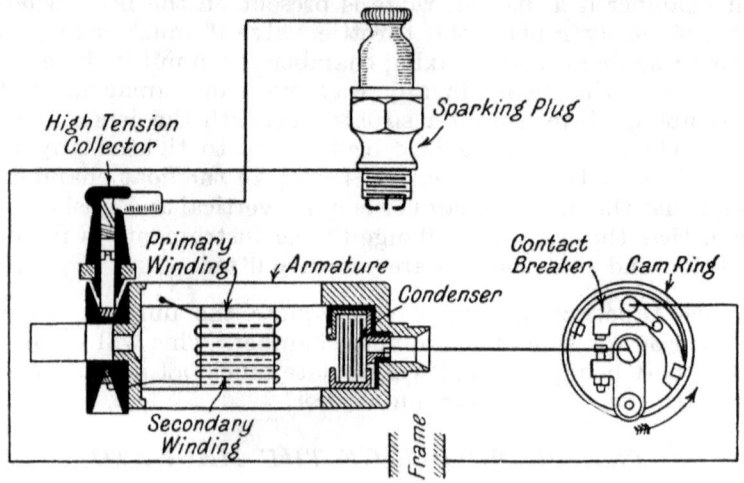

Fig. 24. Magneto Ignition Wiring Diagram

top of the compression stroke, all the other "breaks" (and therefore sparks) will occur at this point also, and thus the engine will go on firing correctly. Besides the "break" being timed to take place when the piston is in a certain position (which we call "timing the magneto," page 44), it must also be timed to occur at the moment when the bobbin is having the greatest effect on the magnetic field. This, of course, is allowed for in the design of the magneto, and does not really concern the reader. Also, it is essential that the primary circuit should be complete (i.e. the contacts must be properly closed) both before and after the "break," which should be of very short duration.

The *cam ring*, against which the cam of the contact breaker works, can be rotated by handlebar control through about 15 degrees, thereby giving means of advancing and retarding the spark. On recent "Magdynos" there is no cam ring (see Fig. 27).

The *condenser* is a device for the purpose of eliminating "arcing," and the *pick-up* is a small carbon brush kept in continual contact with the *slip-ring*, in order to collect or pick up the high tension current for the sparking plug lead.

Magneto ignition (or rather "Magdyno" ignition) is provided on 16 out of the 23 1938 four-strokes.

THE PRINCIPLE OF COIL IGNITION

Coil ignition has many features in common with magneto ignition, but there are certain very distinct variations. Its principal characteristic is that it generates a high-tension current of practically *constant voltage*, and is thus admirably suited for easy starting and efficiency at low engine speeds. On the magneto the

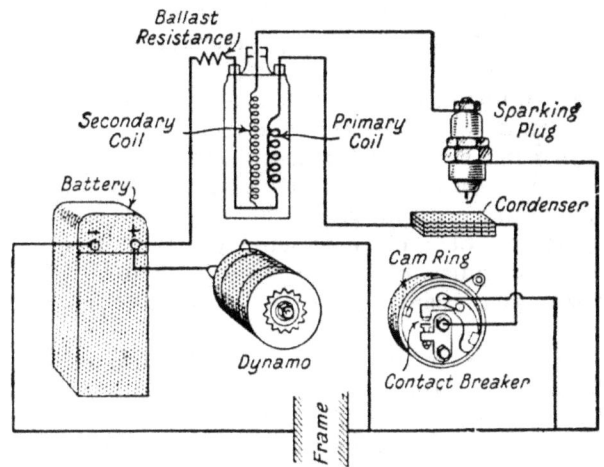

FIG. 25. THE ESSENTIAL COMPONENTS OF COIL IGNITION

On the Royal Enfields a ballast resistance is not used and the contact breaker, which is of a different type to that shown (see Fig. 28) is mounted on the Lucas dynamo.

high-tension current is induced in the secondary winding by the interruption of the primary circuit, which depends for its voltage upon the speed at which the armature is rotating. With coil ignition a low-tension current is generated by a *dynamo* and led straight to a *battery*, from which the current is supplied at a practically fixed voltage to the primary *coil*; and the high-tension current is generated in the secondary coil by induction as on the magneto, a *contact-breaker* with central cam on the dynamo driven at engine speed interrupting the primary circuit at predetermined intervals. Coil ignition is used on 1938 Models A, B, T, S, J, H and on the new Model CO. The system is shown diagrammatically in Fig. 25. It will be observed that in addition to the battery, dynamo, coils, and contact-breaker, there is a *condenser* in series with the contact-breaker as on the magneto. Other features (not shown) are the "tell-tale" warning lamp which shows when the ignition is switched on (see page 49), the dynamo cut-out, which prevents battery discharge to dynamo, and the panel-ignition switch which earths the primary current.

Timing the Ignition. In the event of the "Magdyno" or dynamo (coil ignition models) being removed or the drive disturbed it will be necessary to retime the ignition which is done as follows. Turn the engine until the piston is at the top of the stroke, being careful to observe on 4-stroke models that it is at the top of the compression stroke, i.e. that no valve has opened during the ascent of the piston. Next set the handlebar ignition lever to the fully advanced position. Then rotate the engine backwards (by means of the rear wheel with top gear engaged) until the piston is exactly a distance from top dead centre position corresponding to the correct ignition or spark advance given in a later paragraph. To measure the distance, which varies on different engines from $\frac{1}{16}$ in. to $\frac{3}{8}$ in., the cylinder head should be removed on sidevalve engines, but on the overhead-valve and two-stroke engines it is only necessary to remove the sparking plug and gauge the distance by means of a piece of wire inserted through the plug hole. Two marks must, of course, be scratched on the wire, one indicating top dead centre and the other above it the spark advance.

Some riders prefer to time the ignition by measuring degrees of crankshaft rotation, and in this case a degree disc must be attached to the crankshaft. The author is of the opinion, however, that this method is really "splitting hairs" and quite unnecessary and apt to entail a considerable amount of bother. Measurements taken on the piston stroke are sufficiently accurate as far as ignition timing is concerned for all normal purposes, although in the case of valve timing where extreme accuracy is wanted the degree method of timing is undoubtedly preferable.

Having determined the correct position of the piston when the spark should occur on full advance, it only remains to check that the contact breaker points are beginning to "break" in this position with the spark lever fully advanced. The contacts in this position should not be less or farther apart than will allow a thin piece of tissue paper or cigarette paper to be just freed. If the contacts have not separated or have a wide gap between them, all that is necessary on the coil ignition models is to remove the contact breaker cover (held by a single screw) from the end of the dynamo and slacken the large central screw securing the contact breaker cam to the armature of the dynamo. The contact breaker cam may then be gently turned until the contacts are beginning to break.

On the "Magdyno" models the contact breaker is keyed to its shaft and consequently if it is necessary to retime the ignition, the timing cover must be removed and the armature driving pinion (see Fig. 54) slackened on its taper by loosening the fixing nut.

THE CARBURETTOR AND IGNITION

With the 976 c.c. Big Twin either cylinder may be timed, although it is usual to time the rear one. Afterwards the timing for both cylinders should be checked. The cam for the front cylinder is the one following the longer distance between the two cams. On removing the brush holders a brass segment of the slip ring will be seen through one hole and a fibre segment through the other hole. The lead to the rear cylinder should connect with the brass segment. On the Big Twin the ignition may be timed with the cylinder head removed, but if this is in place, timing can be done by removing the small screwed plug from the centre of the head and inserting a wire through the hole. On this machine it is necessary to slacken the "Magdyno" driving sprocket after removing the chain case cover.

On Model Z "Cycar" access to the flywheel magneto is obtained by removing the black enamelled cover on the off side of the machine. When this is done the flywheel will be seen, while behind the spokes of this is a small round cover secured by a spring clip. Removal of this discloses the contact points, which will be seen to open and close as the flywheel is turned round. In order to time the ignition it is necessary to slacken the flywheel (flywheel ignition is used on this machine) on its taper by loosening the centre nut and turning it to the left until it locks against the flywheel. By turning the nut another turn it causes the flywheel to be pulled off its taper, so enabling the flywheel to be rotated relative to its shaft until the contacts are just beginning to break.

After retiming the ignition always check the timing in case it has been disturbed when tightening the fixing screw or nut as the case may be.

On 1934–5 Models C and L, which have aluminium heads, on no account advance the spark more than $\frac{3}{32}$ in. This is exceedingly important.

Ignition Timings. All the timings given below are with the ignition lever on full advance. On Models A, Z (two-stroke) the contacts should begin to break when the piston is $\frac{1}{8}$ in. to $\frac{3}{16}$ in. before top dead centre (T.D.C.). An advance of $\frac{1}{8}$ in. gives superior hill climbing, but for speed an advance of $\frac{3}{16}$ in. is slightly more satisfactory. On Model T the correct ignition timing is $\frac{5}{16}$ in. before T.D.C. On Models C, CO, K, KX $\frac{3}{8}$ in. before T.D.C. should begiven. On Models H and L the advance should be $\frac{1}{8}$ in. on engines No. 10546 upwards and $\frac{1}{4}$ in. on earlier types. In the case of Models LO, LO2 the correct advance is $\frac{1}{2}$ in. to $\frac{5}{8}$ in. before T.D.C. On Models G and J2 give $\frac{3}{8}$ in. before T.D.C. ($\frac{1}{2}$ in. on J2 4-valve). On the 250, 350 c.c. "Bullets" allow $\frac{1}{2}$ in. before T.D.C. and $\frac{1}{4}$ in. on the 500 c.c. Competition Model and Models J, B. On Models S, S2 to obtain the best results give $\frac{1}{8}$ in.

before T.D.C. On the 1934 Models BO, LF an advance of $\frac{7}{16}$ in. to $\frac{1}{2}$ in. is recommended.

Care of "Magdyno" (Ignition Unit). Little attention is required (for maintenance of dynamo unit, see page 69), and if any serious trouble arises it is best to return the instrument to the makers for attention. Never attempt to remove the armature.

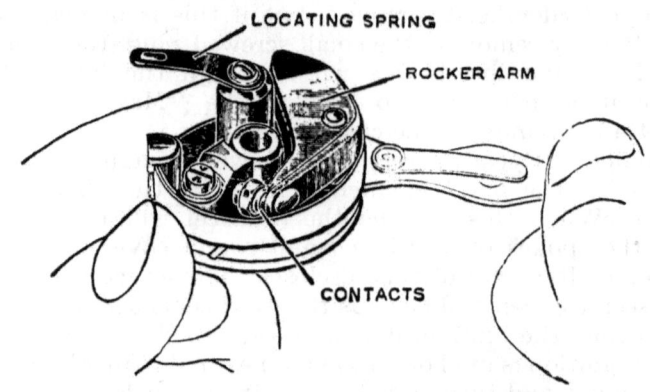

(*Messrs. Joseph Lucas, Ltd.*)

FIG. 26. SHOWING "MAGDYNO" RING CAM CONTACT BREAKER AND METHOD OF REMOVING THE ROCKER ARM

The contact points in the contact breaker should be kept adjusted so that they open to an extent equal to the thickness of the gauge on the magneto spanner (·012 in.). One of the contacts (*E*, Fig. 27) will be found to be adjustable, and care must be taken to slacken the lock nut before attempting to adjust the contact. The contact breaker is designed to run without lubrication, and except for very occasionally putting a spot of oil on the cam wick (see page 64) or the cam ring wick about every 5000 miles, no lubrication is necessary.

Occasionally, if the machine has been kept in a damp place, the fibre bush on which a rocker arm works will swell and cause the arm to stick, causing irregular firing of the engine. If the contacts remain permanently open the engine cannot be started, for no spark at the plug can occur. The best cure is to remove the contact breaker and rocker (see below) and rub the whole of the inside of the rocker bush with the head of a live safety match, which is usually sufficient to effect a cure. In exceptional cases something rougher may be needed.

The contact points themselves must be kept scrupulously clean. On examination after a big mileage the contacts may be

THE CARBURETTOR AND IGNITION

found to have irregular and dull surfaces due to burning (especially if the contacts have not been kept clean and properly adjusted), and if such is found to be the case it is necessary to polish them up, otherwise misfiring and rapid deterioration of the contacts will inevitably follow. To polish up the contacts, use a fine carborundum stone or emery cloth (or a nail file) and with the contact breaker and rocker arm removed polish the contacts until all pitting is removed and the contact surfaces are bright all over. Be careful to keep the surfaces "square" as well as uniform. To remove the contact breaker and rocker arm on a ring cam contact-breaker, proceed as follows—

Withdraw the contact-breaker from its housing by unscrewing the hexagon-headed screw (G, Fig. 37) in the centre by means of the magneto spanner. The complete contact breaker can then be pulled off the tapered end of the armature to which it is keyed. Next push aside the locating spring and with the magneto spanner prise off the rocker arm from its bearings as shown on Fig. 26.

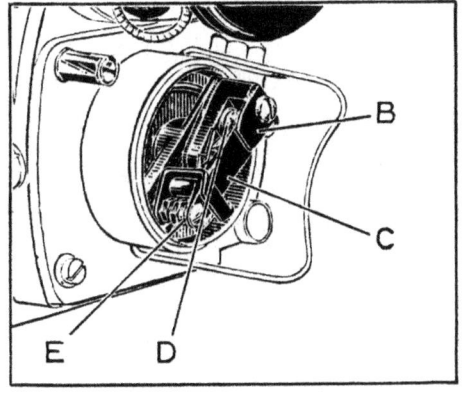

FIG. 27. THE FACE CAM CONTACT BREAKER USED ON PRESENT "MAG-DYNOS"

B = Backing Spring D = Screw for wick
C = Contact spring E = Contacts

After polishing the contacts wipe away all traces of dirt and metal dust with a rag moistened in petrol. When refitting the contact breaker be very careful to see that it engages the keyway on the end of the armature properly, otherwise the ignition timing may be upset.

To remove the spring arm carrying the moving contact on a face cam type contact breaker (Fig. 27), it is only necessary to withdraw the securing screw. It is important when replacing the arm to make sure that the small backing spring is replaced immediately under the securing screw and spring washer, with the bent part facing outwards.

Occasionally remove the H.T. pick-up (there are two on Model K) and examine the carbon brush. It should work freely in its guide and not be unduly worn. When examining the brush avoid stretching the pick-up brush spring unduly, or a new one will be required. Renew both the brush and spring if they are in questionable condition. Also occasionally clean the slip ring track and flanges by inserting a small rag wrapped round a pencil through the pick-up hole and slowly revolving the engine. Little attention is required in regard to lubrication of the armature bearings, and this is referred to on page 64.

The Dynamo Contact Breaker (Coil Ignition). Occasionally remove the moulded cover and inspect the contact breake which is illustrated in Fig. 28. The contacts must be kept quite clean and free from grease or oil. If burned or blackened, polish the contacts as in the case of the "Magdyno" with fine carborundum stone or emery cloth and afterwards wipe quite clean with a petrol-moistened rag. If much attention is necessary to the contacts it is best to remove the rocker arm from its housing. After removing the nut and collar securing the rocker arm spring the rocker arm can be lifted clear of its pin. Finally after polishing and cleaning the contacts refit the rocker arm, replace the collar and nut, and check the gap between the contacts.

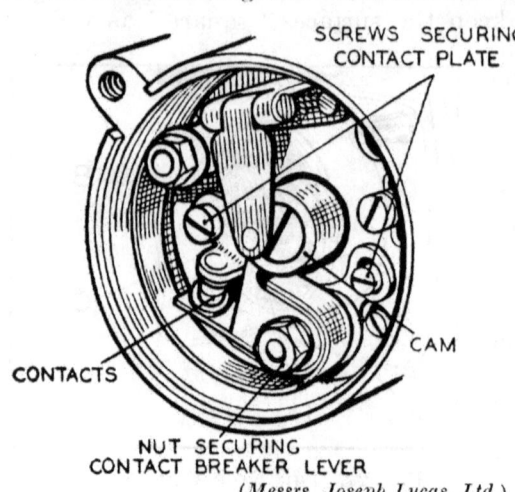

FIG. 28. THE DYNAMO CONTACT BREAKER (COIL IGNITION MODELS)

(*Messrs. Joseph Lucas, Ltd.*)

The contact breaker gap should be maintained at 8 to 10 thousandths of an inch, and to test the gap which requires adjustment only at long intervals, slowly revolve the engine by hand until the contacts are wide open. Then insert between the contacts the magneto spanner gauge which should just slide in. If the gap is considerably too large or too small, adjust by opening the contacts fully and then slackening the locking screws until the plate carrying the stationary contact can just be moved. Now adjust the position of the plate until the correct gap at the contacts is obtained. Afterwards the locking screws may be retightened and the gap again checked.

When refitting the moulded cover it is important to see that the hinged steel blade on the contact breaker makes good contact with the condenser case within the cover. If the blade fails to press firmly against the case, sparking at the contacts will occur and the contacts will suffer considerably.

THE CARBURETTOR AND IGNITION

What the Ignition Warning Lamp is For. Its object is to show when the ignition is switched on, as on coil ignition models it is important to disconnect the battery from the coil when the machine is left standing. As soon as the engine revolutions are high enough to cause the dynamo to begin charging, the warning lamp goes out. Should the bulb burn out, the running of the machine is in no way affected, but the bulb should be replaced as soon as possible by a 2·5 volt, ·2 amp. bulb, otherwise the ignition may inadvertently be left switched on for a long time with the machine idle and the battery may become exhausted (see notes on page 76).

Use the Correct Type of Plug. Care should be taken always to use a plug of a type suitable for the engine, as much bother and possibly some damage may be caused through the use of the wrong type or inferior quality plugs. Lodge and K.L.G. sparking plugs are recommended for all Royal Enfield machines; Lodge are fitted as standard.

On side-valve engines with 18 mm. plugs it is best for running-in and ordinary touring to fit a Lodge TS3 or a K.L.G. 777; for prolonged high speed running, fit a Lodge H1 or a K.L.G. 843. Where 14 mm. plugs are provided, suitable plugs to use are the Lodge C14 or the K.L.G. L777 for running-in and ordinary touring, and the Lodge H14 or K.L.G. 831 for prolonged high speed.

In the case of earlier type overhead-valve engines having 18 mm. plugs it is satisfactory to use a Lodge H1 for touring and a Lodge H45 for fast driving. All recent engines have 14 mm. plugs and suitable types to use are the Lodge H14 or K.L.G. 831 for running-in and ordinary touring and the Lodge H53 or K.L.G. L583 for prolonged fast running.

For the two-stroke models a plug should be chosen the electrodes of which are of a considerable size, for the plug of a two-stroke engine has to stand a lot of heat, and thin electrodes are liable to get hot quickly and cause pre-ignition. Sparking plugs suitable for Models A and Z "Cycar" are a Lodge H1 for

Fig. 29. Sectional View of Lodge Sparking Plug

ordinary touring purposes and a Lodge H45 when the engine is continually subjected to very hard work. Corresponding plugs in the K.L.G. range are the KS5 and the 583 respectively.

Tending the Plug. Difficult starting or occasional misfiring may often be traced to a dirty or defective plug. The life of a good plug is considerable, but the points of the electrodes gradually burn away and the gap between them becomes enlarged considerably. For this reason it is advisable occasionally to check the gap at the electrodes with a feeler gauge. The correct gap is ·018 in. with "Magdyno" ignition and ·025 in. with coil ignition. Excessive gap at the plug electrodes is apt to cause difficult starting, especially on the "Magdyno" models where the voltage varies with engine speed, and the raising of the voltage to jump the large gap may cause brush discharge within the magneto portion of the "Magdyno." This discharge is liable to cause internal corrosion and to impair the efficiency of the instrument.

From time to time the plug should be removed, dismantled and thoroughly cleaned with petrol and a wire brush, both inside and outside. All carbon and soot deposits should be removed. Clean the mica insulation only with a rag soaked in petrol. Examine the plug insulation for signs of burning or flaking and if a waterproof terminal is not fitted, fit one.

Note to 1937-8 " R.E." Owners. Most 1937-8 Royal Enfields have automatic voltage control (see page 81) and it is useful to remember that with this equipment it is possible to run with the lights on and the battery disconnected without risk of "blowing" the bulbs. If the battery is disconnected, the positive lead to it should be taped up, not earthed. A coil ignition model may be started with the battery disconnected by running the machine hard in bottom gear. When the engine starts the exhausted battery may be reconnected.

Testing It. The usual method of testing for H.T. current at the plug terminal is to bridge the terminal and the cylinder head with the steel blade of a *wooden-handled* screwdriver, when a spark should be visible on rotating the engine. To test the plug itself, remove it with the H.T. lead attached, clean it, lay it on the cylinder (with the terminal clear of the head) and ascertain whether it sparks satisfactorily with the engine rotated. In daylight the spark is not bright, but it should be distinctly heard. Another way of testing the plug is to use a pencil type neon tube plug tester which can be obtained cheaply from accessory dealers.

CHAPTER V

ALL ABOUT LUBRICATION

THE lubrication system on Royal Enfields has been steadily improved during recent years and all present single-cylinder models with, of course, the exception of the two-stroke models incorporate the most modern type of automatic dry sump engine

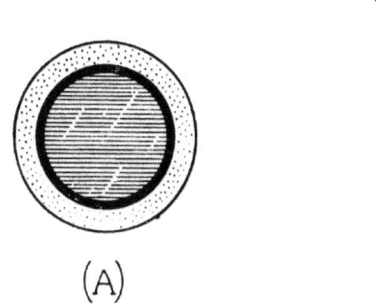 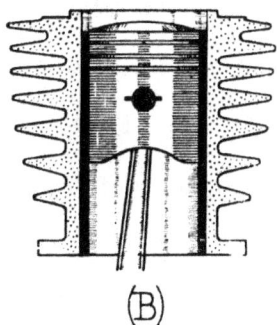

(A) (B)

FIG. 30. SHOWING GENERAL PRINCIPLE OF LUBRICATION
The diagrams at A and B show how an oil film keeps a shaft apart from its bearing and a piston apart from its cylinder respectively.

lubrication system, ensuring correct lubrication of all the working parts with the minimum amount of attention. Some attention on the part of the rider is, however, necessary and can never safely be neglected if a host of evil troubles is to be avoided. Motorcycling can be cheap, but it can also with neglect be quite the reverse.

What Lubrication Is For. The fundamental principle of lubrication is that to avoid friction and heat, or in other words wear and tear, between close-fitting moving surfaces it is imperative to maintain an oil or grease film between them, which does in effect actually keep them apart. The idea is made clear in Fig. 30. On a motor-cycle the oil film has a thickness varying from about ·0002 in. to ·0008 in. and the duty of the rider in regard to engine lubrication is to see that: (a) good quality oil is used, (b) a sufficient quantity of oil is kept in circulation, (c) the oil is kept clean and free from dilution (petrol gradually creeps past the piston rings).

Suitable Engine Oils to Use. "Any old oil" will definitely not do and the use of an unsuitable oil is false economy in the widest sense. Always purchase engine oil from branded cabinets or sealed cans and ask for the correct grade *and* brand of oil and *see that you get it.* Engine oils recommended for replenishing the tank or crankcase reservoir as the case may be (including the two-strokes) are Patent Castrol XXL, Mobiloil D, Golden Shell (Extra Heavy), or Essolube Racer. These oils flow freely when cold and possess excellent heat-resisting properties.

For Competition Work use Patent Castrol R, Mobiloil R, or Shell Super Heavy oil for the engine. These oils have a vegetable base, and stand extreme heat conditions better than the oils recommended for ordinary use. These special oils must not, however, be mixed with oils recommended above, or with any mineral-base oil. When changing from one type of oil to the other, the engine and tank must be drained and preferably taken apart and cleaned.

MECHANICAL PUMP LUBRICATION

This type of wet sump lubrication system is employed on the twin-cylinder 1934–6 Model K. Oil is carried in a separate compartment at the rear of the petrol tank and is fed by gravity to the mechanical pump from a pipe leading from the off side of the tank. No tap is incorporated on the oil pipe union as this is quite unnecessary (when they were fitted they used to be forgotten!), but a suitable gauze filter is provided above the union and should occasionally be removed and cleaned.

The Pilgrim Type G1 Pump. The mechanical pump which is a Pilgrim type G1 with sight feed, made by the Pilgrim Way Motor Co., Ltd., of Farnham, Surrey, is of the oscillating plunger type with hand-controlled regulator on the right-hand side. It is driven by a coupling from the camshaft and is mounted on the outside of the "Magdyno" driving chain case in a very accessible position. The pump which is shown sectioned in Fig. 31 does not rely on gravity or crankcase suction to get the oil out of the sight feed chamber. The oil is sucked out by the pump and forced through to the engine under considerable pressure. Oil is pumped through a small pipe leading from the delivery side of the pump to a point mid-way between the bases of the cylinders and traverses an horizontal passage leading to the base of the front cylinder, where it is picked up by the piston skirt and thoroughly lubricates the front cylinder. Surplus oil falls to the base of the sump and is splashed by the flywheels on to the rear cylinder, big-ends and

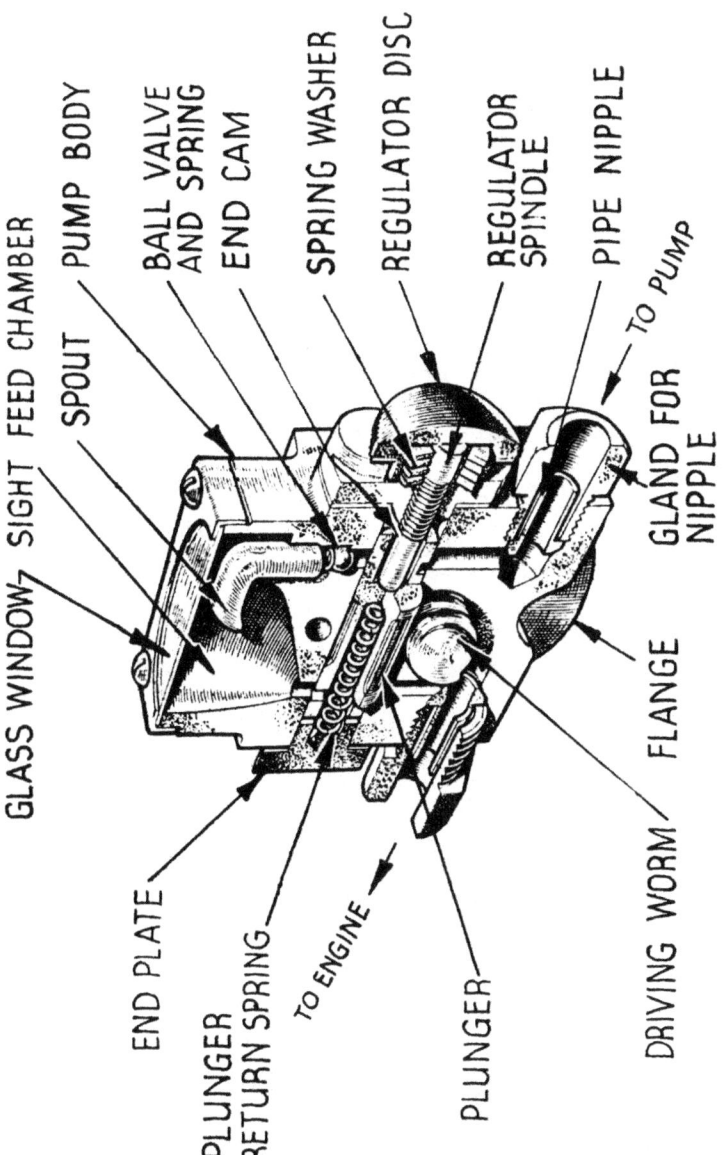

Fig. 31. Sectional View of Pilgrim Mechanical Pump
(*By courtesy of Messrs. Shell-Mex & B.P. Ltd.*)
This single-acting pump is fitted to 1934–36 Model K only and is driven from the camshaft extension.

mainshaft bearings. The timing gear is lubricated by oil mist blown into the timing case where the oil is kept at a fixed level by holes communicating with the crankcase.

Referring to Fig. 31, the action of the Pilgrim pump can be readily understood. The worm on the driving spindle which is coupled to the camshaft rotates the plunger which has longitudinal teeth and since the plunger which has a projection on the right-hand end is kept up against the face of the end cam by means of a return spring, an oscillating as well as a rotary motion is imparted to the plunger, and the two ports in the plunger are timed to operate at the correct moments, passing along a supply of oil in drops past a non-return ball valve and past the beak or spout of the sight feed and then down past the second port into the pipe leading to the engine. The supply of oil fed to the engine is capable of being altered over quite a big range by means of the hand regulator disc on the right-hand side of the pump body. This regulator alters the capacity of the ports.

To Obtain the Correct Setting. On taking delivery of a new Big Twin the Pilgrim pump should be very carefully regulated. First set the engine controls until the engine is gently ticking-over. Then cut the oil supply right off temporarily by rotating the regulator disc *clockwise* as far as it will go and afterwards rotate in the reverse direction until oil just begins to be delivered by the pump, which can be ascertained at the sight feed glass window. Now further rotate the regulator three or four numbered divisions (there are four notches to a numbered division) beyond this point and the pump will be set to deliver a fairly generous supply of oil suitable for running-in purposes (see page 65). Probably it will be found that the above setting causes plenty of blue smoke from the exhaust and a rather uneconomical oil consumption. It serves, however, as a reliable jumping off point for ultimately arriving at a satisfactory setting for all-round purposes.

Watch the Sight Feed. An idea of the correct setting may be obtained by watching the oil flow past the sight feed. With a rather generous supply a regular series of oil drops can be seen being delivered by the pump. On rotating the regulator clockwise, the pulsations of oil from the beak or spout still occur at the same intervals, but it will be found that it now takes two, three, or perhaps four or more pulsations to cause a spot of oil large enough to detach itself from the spout and run away from the bottom of the sight feed chamber.

As a rough guide on a new Model K set the Pilgrim pump so that each pulsation just forms a spot of oil big enough to

ALL ABOUT LUBRICATION

detach itself. This may be reduced when running-in is completed to a spot for every two pulsations. Generally speaking, however, the wisest course is to regard the sight feed only as an indication that the pump is working and to arrive at the final setting by observing the exhaust and noting the fuel consumption.

What is the Exhaust Like? The exhaust on a new machine should always be slightly tinged with blue smoke. After running-in the oil supply should be cut down until there is just a slight blue haze at the exhaust when the engine is accelerated quickly in neutral, but not when running under load. If the engine smokes heavily and it is decided to reduce the oil supply, do so one or two notches at a time (four notches equal one division) and proceed several miles before further reducing the oil supply. Generally it takes four to five miles in order for the excess oil in the crankcase to be got rid of.

If In Doubt. Always give too much oil rather than too little. No harm can be done by over lubrication other than bringing the time for decarbonizing nearer, but by under lubrication you may ruin a good engine and afterwards be smitten by remorse. When driving at high speed on prolonged gradients of a stiffish character, increase the oil supply by turning the regulator two or three notches in an anti-clockwise direction.

Oil Consumption as a Guide. On Model K, 100 to 150 miles per pint is the oil consumption to aim at when the machine is properly run in. But bear in mind that on an engine which has seen a great deal of service the bearings may be somewhat on the slack side and wastage of oil may make it unsafe to adjust the pump to give a consumption of oil as low as mentioned above.

What to Do if the Sight Feed Fills Up. Occasional filling up of the sight feed in cold weather may be due merely to the viscous state of the oil and the remedy is to increase the supply of oil for a short time, when the trouble will probably cure itself.

In the event of any small particle of dirt or foreign matter lodging between the ball valve and its seat, the sight feed will fill up with oil when standing, and the ball valve should be attended to. This valve (Fig. 31) is situated in the body of the pump underneath the spout, and the ball, spring, valve seat and passages should be thoroughly cleaned. To do this it is necessary to unscrew the glass window and then with a pair of flat-nosed pliers remove the spout or beak, which is a tight push fit in the body of the pump.

Chronic and regular filling up of the sight feed under all

conditions of temperature and oil may be due to wear of the end cam, and the remedy is obvious; fit a new part (see Fig. 32).

If the Glass Breaks. This will in no way interfere with the working of the pump, but the author would stress the need for using common sense in this eventuality and covering up the window with a piece of stiff paper or other suitable material. If dirt gets into the sight feed chamber it will cause trouble as has already been mentioned.

Some Possible Causes of Irregular Pump Action. Trouble seldom occurs with the Pilgrim pump, but if oil is passed irregularly or the supply of oil falls off at high speed, look to the following three points—

(a) Examine and if necessary clean the gauze filter above the tank union. See that the level of oil in the tank is not so low as to prevent the filter being completely immersed, otherwise air instead of petrol may be passed to the pump and engine.

(b) See that there are no particles of fluff or dirt obstructing the action of the ball valve or any of the passages. For remedy, see paragraph relating to filling up of the sight feed chamber.

(c) Check that there are no air leaks on the inlet side of the pump and that all pipe unions are tight. Test them with a spanner but do not be "ham fisted."

Dismantling Pilgrim Pump. This is rarely necessary, but if you must take it to bits first and foremost unscrew the worm driving spindle bush (R.H. thread) and remove the worm and spindle. Until this has been done you must on no account remove or attempt to remove the plunger. The penalty is expensive damage! It should also be noted that it is dangerous to revolve the worm with either the end plate or the end cam (see Fig. 32) removed from the body of the pump. After removing the worm, remove the end plate and withdraw the plunger. When reassembling first fit the end cam (if this has been removed) and then the plunger should be inserted cam first, so that the two cams are in contact with each other. Then replace the return spring in the open end of the plunger (i.e. the end with the longest hole) and box it in with the end plate. It now remains to complete assembly by inserting the worm and screwing in the spindle bush.

After Draining Crankcase. After draining the crankcase it is necessary to pour oil over the flywheels before starting up, as it is impossible for the Pilgrim pump to deliver a large supply of oil immediately. Draining should be carried out when decarbonizing

ALL ABOUT LUBRICATION 57

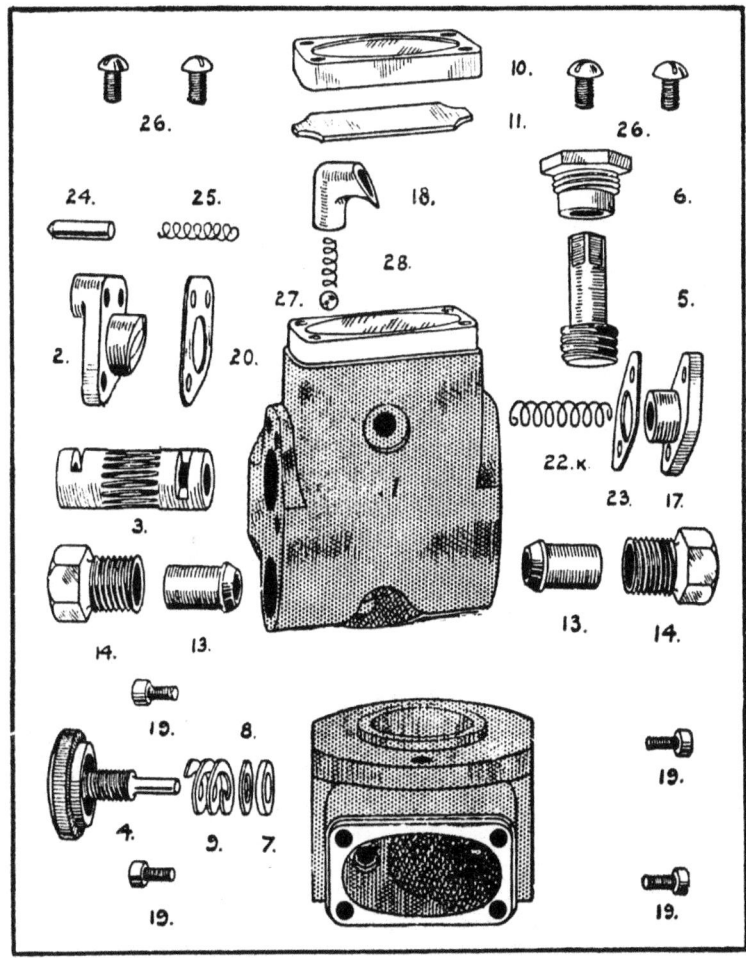

(*Pilgrim Way Motor Co., Ltd.*)

FIG. 32. THE PILGRIM TYPE G1 PUMP COMPLETELY DISMANTLED

The above illustration (see also Fig. 31) should prove useful if you need to refit any new parts, as the numbers in the key are the makers' part numbers.

KEY TO FIG. 32

1. Pump body
2. End cam
3. Plunger
4. Regulator and spindle
5. Driving worm and spindle
6. Bush for worm spindle
7. Fibre washer
8. Steel washer
9. Spring washer
10. Window frame
11. Glass window
13. Pipe nipple
14. Gland for nipple
17. End plate
18. Beak or spout
19. Cam and end plate screws
20. Cam washer
22K. Plunger return spring
23. End plate washer
24. Ratchet
25. Ratchet spring
26. Window frame screw
27. Ball valve
28. Ball valve spring

and at the end of a run when the oil is warm. Flush out with petrol.

PETROIL LUBRICATION

This system of engine lubrication is used on the two-stroke models (A, Z) only and is extremely simple in principle and application. On the two-stroke engine the cycle of operations (page 27) entails the admission and compression of the petrol vapour in the crankcase and this with a mechanical pump or dry sump system of lubrication would render lubrication of the big-end and main shaft bearings very hazardous and generally unsatisfactory. The difficulty is overcome in a childishly simple manner with the petroil system by replenishing the tank with a mixture of oil and petrol in certain definite proportions.

The Proportions of Oil and Petrol to Use. For normal use replenish the tank with a mixture consisting of *one part of oil to sixteen of petrol*, or in other words add half a pint of oil to each gallon of petrol. During the running-in period, however, slightly more oil should be used and the author recommends the mixing of three-quarters of a pint with each gallon of petrol. Always use a good quality oil of a kind suitable for the engine (see page 52).

Mixing the Petroil. All Royal Enfield two-strokes have a measure attached to the underside of the tank filler cap and as four full measures exactly equals half a pint, there is no necessity to scrounge round for a half pint glass measure when replenishing. It will be noticed that on the filler cap measure the rider is instructed to use *five* measures, but this applies only during running-in. Afterwards it is quite sufficient to mix *four* measures of engine oil with each gallon of petrol. The best petrol to use, incidentally, is a good No. 1 brand. Do not use benzole-mixture, as this is not recommended for two-stroke engines although in the case of high compression overhead-valve engines its use has many advantages and gives good results.

Shake or Stir the Mixture Well. Before pouring the petroil mixture into the tank it should be stirred or shaken well in a separate vessel. Always make a habit of doing this, because if the mixture is poured straight into the tank there is a considerable risk of trouble arising due to the oil settling at the bottom of the tank.

In Cold Weather. It will facilitate restarting, particularly in cold weather, if the petrol tap is turned off *before* stopping so as to drain the carburettor. This prevents oil collecting in the jets and possibly choking them.

ALL ABOUT LUBRICATION 59

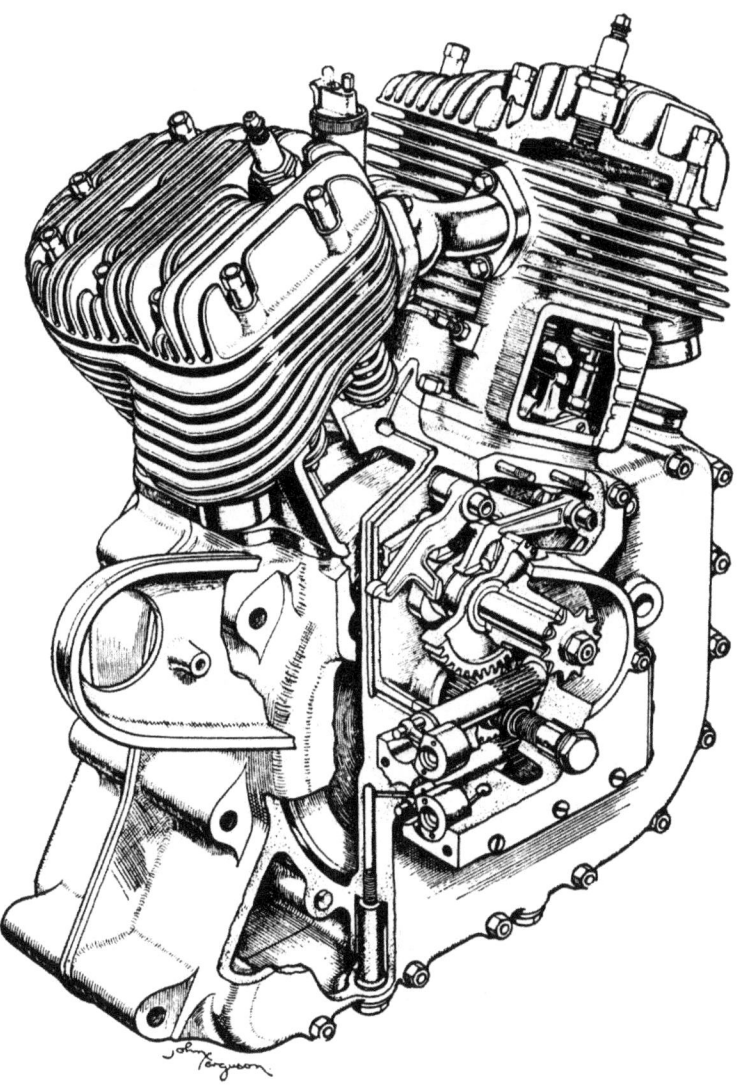

(*From "The Motor Cycle"*)

FIG. 33. SHOWING THE TWIN OIL PUMPS AND OTHER DETAILS OF THE 1140 C.C. SIDE-VALVE ENGINE FITTED TO THE 1937–8 MODELS K AND KX

A diagram of the dry sump lubrication system is given on page 63. Prior to 1937 mechanical pump lubrication was used.

60 BOOK OF THE ROYAL ENFIELD

DRY SUMP LUBRICATION

All 1934-8 Singles. A true dry sump system of lubrication is used in which the whole of the oil is kept in constant circulation by a double-acting plunger type oil pump housed at the foot of the timing case and worm-driven off the engine main shaft.

The oil in the "sump," or portion of the crankcase below the

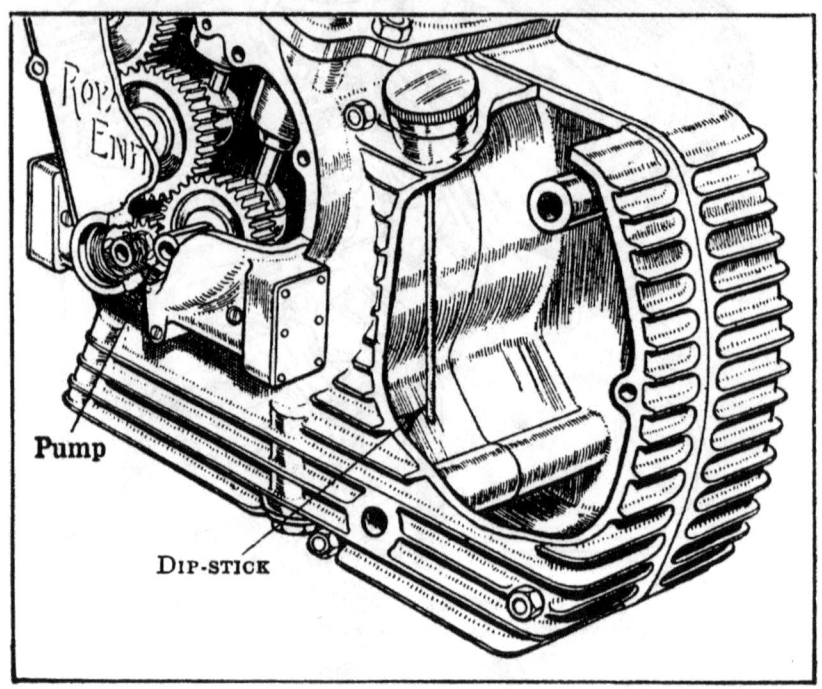

(*From "The Motor Cycle"*)

Fig. 34. Showing the Interior of the Oil Reservoir or Tank and the Arrangement of the Double-acting Oil Pump
The pump is worm-driven from an extension of the main shaft. The oil return pipe is not visible. A 1935 engine is shown.

flywheels, is kept at a level below the bottom of the flywheels, so that these do not dip. The main supply of oil is carried in an oil tank formed in the crankcase casting. This tank has a capacity of over three pints, which is sufficient for approximately 500 miles running. The oil is sucked from the tank by the oil feed pump, through the oil filter, and is delivered by the oil feed nozzle into the timing side shaft of the engine. From this point it is flung by centrifugal force through a passage in the web of the flywheel to the big-end, from which it is flung on to the walls of the cylinder. Large holes in the partition separating the crankcase from the timing case enable the oil spray to pass through to the latter,

ALL ABOUT LUBRICATION

where the oil is held at a suitable level by means of drain holes leading back to the crankcase. Special passages are formed, ensuring an adequate supply of oil to the timing side and driving, side main bearings and to the camshaft bearings. On 1938 "R.E." engines oil is fed by the return oil pump to the timing case and is pumped back to the oil reservoir by the two intermediate gears in the magneto drive.

On the 1934-5 overhead-valve engines (Models G, BO, LF, T) crankcase pressure is used to blow oil mist up the push-rod tunnels to lubricate the push-rod ends and in the case of the last three machines mentioned above, the overhead rockers and valve guides also. Grease gun nipples are, however, provided on Models G, BO, LF to supplement the oil mist lubrication of the overhead valve gear. On some 1935-6 and all the 1937-8 (except J2 4-valve) overhead-valve engines a spring-loaded ball valve is incorporated in the delivery passage from the return pump and some of the oil is diverted to lubricate positively the whole of the overhead valve gear. This oil drains eventually by gravity.

On certain 1937-8 O.H.V. engines (the 250 and 350 c.c. "Bullets") a check valve is fitted below the lower oil pipe union to prevent excessive oil reaching the semi-enclosed rocker housing.

After circulating round the working parts of the engine the oil collects in the sump and is sucked through the oil return filter (the second of two filters incorporated in the system) by the oil return pump, which is slightly larger than the feed pump, and delivered to the tank by the oil return passage. This passage is visible on removing the oil filler cap and the return of oil issuing out of it provides an indication that the dry sump lubrication system is functioning satisfactorily.

1937-8 Big Twins.

As on the S.V. and O.H.V. singles, a true dry sump lubrication system is provided and it has many features in common with that described above. The oil in the "sump" or crankcase compartment (which has a capacity of over 7 pints) is kept at a level below the flywheels so that they cannot dip. No means of adjusting the oil feed is provided, oil being fed liberally to the big-end, the front cylinder and the timing gears; surplus oil is returned to the "sump" for further circulation.

Referring to Fig. 35, the main oil supply is contained in the oil tank A which constitutes part of the crankcase casting and is sucked up by the two feed pumps B and C (at the rear end of the timing cover) through the filter D. Oil is delivered by pump B to the big-end and is then splashed over the cylinders and piston; some of it is also led to the main bearings along special ducts. An auxiliary oil supply is fed by pump C (which is smaller than B) to the front cylinder which on twin-cylinder engines tends to receive less oil than the rear one. Surplus oil accumulates in the sumps E, E at the base of the crankcase and is then sucked up by the first return pump F (which has a capacity greater than the combined capacity of B and C) through a filter G and delivered to the timing case. Oil is drawn from a high level in the timing case by the second return pump H (which is of the same size as F) and returned to the main oil tank or "sump" A. This briefly is the working of the D.S. lubrication system used on Models K and KX.

If the Oil Pumps are Stripped Down, see that they are assembled correctly—the larger plunger goes in the return pump, which is the one in front of the timing cover. Do not omit the spring washer between the pump disc and the cover plate. This is essential to the correct functioning of the pumps.

Replenish Tank Regularly. Bear this in mind: If the tank becomes completely empty the engine is with the dry sump lubrication system entirely starved of oil and it is only a question of a short time before it "goes west." To be on the safe side, frequently remove the filler cap and with the dip-stick attached to the underside ascertain the oil level and replenish with suitable engine oil (see page 52) if necessary. The oil level must always be kept above the end of the dip-stick and the tank should not be replenished beyond the mark near the top end of the stick, otherwise oil may escape down the air vent leading to the primary chain on non-oilbath models. It should not be forgotten that the more oil there is in circulation, the cooler will it be. The tank, as may be seen in Fig. 34, is situated right at the front to assist cooling.

To Verify Oil Circulation. Remove the tank filler cap and peer inside when if all is well the oil can be seen issuing from the oil return pipe in a uniform series of drops.

Warm Engine Up Gradually. Some riders as soon as they have started the engine proceed to race it, presumably with the idea of impressing bystanders of the powerful mount they are about to ride. This apart from the question of ethics is thoroughly bad practice and is proof of ignorance, for until the engine oil reaches a certain temperature it will not be circulating with maximum efficiency. On the other hand, do not let the engine tick over too slowly when warming up because this reduces the speed of oil circulation, possibly to a dangerous extent when the oil is in a very viscous state.

Drain Oil Tank and Refill with Fresh Oil About Every 1500-2000 Miles. About every 1500 to 2000 miles the oil should be

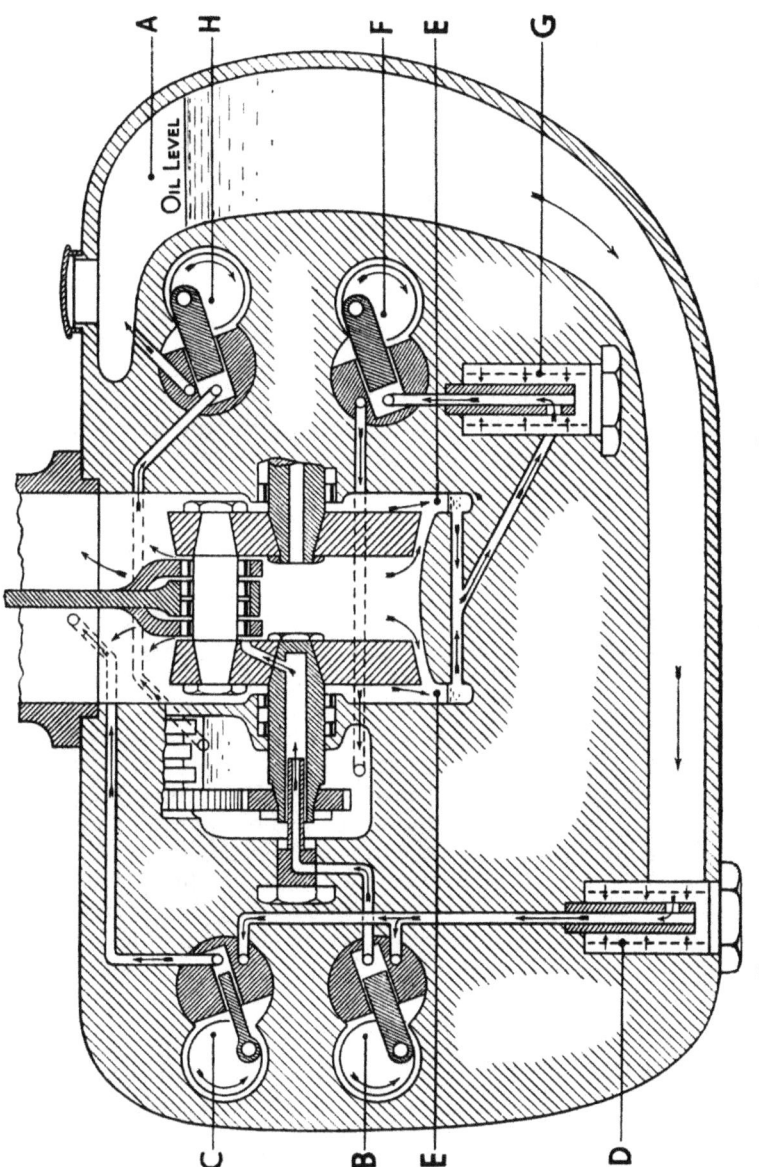

FIG. 35. DIAGRAM OF 1937–8 TWIN-CYLINDER LUBRICATION SYSTEM

drained from the tank and the sump by removing the two filter plugs. (The rear plug drains the tank, and the front one the sump.) The filter gauzes should be brushed with paraffin to clean them and the tank and sump swilled through with petrol, allowed to drain, and refilled with fresh oil. This procedure is conveniently carried out when the machine is being decarbonized. The oil will flow more readily if the plugs are removed at the conclusion of a ride, or the tank and sump may be allowed to drain over night. Waste of oil is reduced by allowing the oil level in the tank to become *reasonably* low before draining.

Grease Overhead Valve Gear About Every 300 Miles. On 1934-6 O.H.V. engines where positive lubrication of the overhead valve gear is not provided, the grease nipples provided for supplementing the oil mist lubrication should have the grease gun applied to them about every 300 miles, or about once a week. When applying the grease gun continue injecting grease until it begins to exude from the bearings. For valve gear lubrication use a good heat-resisting grease, such as Price's H.M.P.

As already stated, 1937-8 O.H.V. engines have a positive feed to the rocker gear and push-rods, and no attention or adjustment is necessary.

" Magdyno " Lubrication. Every Lucas "Magdyno" during assembly has the bearings and gear wheels packed with grease, and for this reason no lubricators are provided on the instrument. After many thousands of miles running, however, the "Magdyno" should be returned to the makers for dismantling, cleaning, and repacking of the bearings with grease.

In order, however, to minimize wear of the fibre heel of the contact breaker, provision is made for the oiling of the cam ring. A pocket in the contact breaker housing contains a length of felt soaked in oil, and in the cam ring there is a hole filled with a wick to enable the oil to find its way on to the cam ring surface. It is advisable every 5000 miles to withdraw the cam ring and place a few drops of *thin* oil on the felt. If this is done it will be found that the magneto will run for long periods without it being necessary to adjust the gap between the contacts.

The Latest " Magdyno." The ignition portion now has a face cam type contact breaker (Fig. 27) and the cam is lubricated by a wick in the base of the contact breaker. A few drops of thin machine oil should be added about every 5000 miles. By removing the spring arm carrying the moving contact the wick screw can be withdrawn. On some "Magdynos" a lubricator is provided on the commutator end bracket and a few drops of thin oil should be added every 4000-5000 miles.

Dynamo Lubrication (Coil Ignition). The armature bearings are packed with grease on assembly as in the case of the "Magdyno" and the preceding remarks apply here also. The contact breaker, however, requires just a little attention. Every 5000 miles apply a single drop of oil to the pivot (Fig. 28) on which the rocker arm works. Also, with a little Mobilgrease No. 2 lightly smear the surface of the steel cam about every 1000 miles.

Colloidal Graphite for Running-in. The mixing of Acheson's Colloidal Graphite with engine oil in the proportion of one pint to a gallon of oil is strongly advocated during the running-in period. It protects the bearing faces from metal pick-up and makes for cooler running; it also is beneficial to the valves. The compound is obtainable from most garages and it is a good plan to continue to use it even when the running-in period has been completed. In this case the quantity used can be reduced by one-half.

LUBRICATION OF CYCLE PARTS

The results obtained from a well tuned and lubricated engine can be marred considerably unless due attention is paid to the lubrication of the cycle parts, particularly the gearbox and transmission.

Four-speed Gearbox Lubrication. The level of oil in the four-speed gearbox used on all 1934-5 models except the two-strokes should be checked about every 500 miles by means of the dipstick attached to the oil tank filler cap and if necessary replenished with suitable engine oil (see page 52). Always keep the gearbox approximately *half full* of engine oil. Do not on any account replenish with heavy grease, or the gears may suffer damage on account of receiving insufficient lubrication. On 1936-8 models with four-speed gearboxes, check the oil level every 500 to 1000 miles and top up with engine oil to the level of the filling orifice.

Three-speed Gearbox Lubrication. On original assembly the three-speed gearbox fitted on the two-stroke models is filled with a special grease known as "Castrolease Light," but subsequent replenishment should not be undertaken with this lubricant. About every 500 miles remove the filler plug on the right-hand side and top up to the level of the filling orifice with engine oil (see page 52).

If preferred, Castrolease (Light), Mobilgrease (No. 2), or Shell Motor Grease (Soft) may be added to the engine oil.

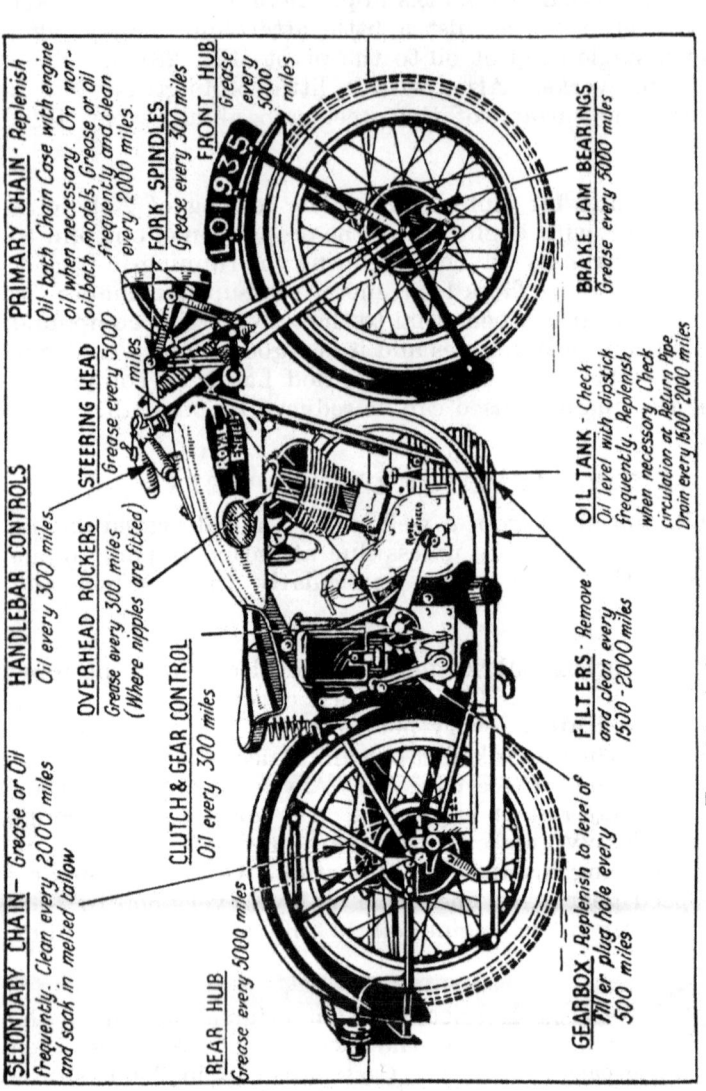

Fig. 36. A Guide to Correct Lubrication

The above chart showing the three-valve Model LO explains when and where to lubricate, and is applicable in general to the whole Royal Enfield range. You will not do any harm if you err slightly from the above recommendations and it is intended to serve as a useful guide to correct lubrication rather than to be meticulously complied with. On the side-valve models there is, of course, no overhead valve gear to lubricate, and on the 1934-6 twin-cylinder model, two-strokes mechanical pump and petroil lubrication are used respectively. It is a good plan when using the grease gun to go over the various nuts with a spanner at the same time.

ALL ABOUT LUBRICATION

Replenish Oil-bath Chain Case when Necessary. On models having the primary chain enclosed in an oil-bath chain case, top up the oil-bath when necessary with engine oil (page 52) to the level of the lower edge of the overflow plug. The chain will then be kept clean and efficiently lubricated, giving a sweet-running and quiet transmission.

On Model Z "Cycar" pour in the first instance about a quarter of a pint of engine oil (page 52) into the chain case through the filler plug and occasionally add a little to compensate for wastage.

Where No Chain Case is Fitted. The primary chain receives a certain amount of lubrication from the breather in the oil tank (except on Model A two-stroke), but this lubrication should frequently be supplemented by applying additional engine oil or grease, especially if the level of oil in the tank is not maintained high. On the two-stroke model mentioned, inspect the chain whenever setting out for a run and lubricate with engine oil or grease if the chain is at all dry.

About every 2000 miles remove the primary chain, wash it thoroughly in paraffin and then allow to soak in melted tallow. This treatment ensures every single one of the links and rollers being adequately lubricated. Remember, the primary chain runs very, very fast and must *not* be neglected.

Lubrication of Secondary Chain. Keep this chain well lubricated with engine oil or grease by frequently applying an oil can to the chain run or smearing it with grease applied to the finger. Although a chain guard is provided, this is insufficient to prevent the chain picking up road filth in dirty weather, and the chain should be dealt with about every 2000 miles in the manner described above for the primary chain.

Grease Wheel Hubs about every 5000 Miles. Apply a good thin grease such as "Castrolease Heavy" to the nipples on the front and rear hubs about every 5000 miles. Be careful not to inject excessive grease, otherwise it may find its way gradually on to the brake linings and you may find that your mount is inclined to run away with you in awkward circumstances.

Also Grease at the same time—the brake cam bearings and the steering head bearings. See that the steering is not stiff. If it is, perhaps the bearings need adjusting (see page 103).

Every 300 Miles.—Grease the fork spindles, rear brake pedal; apply a little oil to the handlebar controls, external gear and clutch control mechanism, etc., about every 300 miles. It is quite surprising how just that little extra attention "makes all the difference."

Suitable Greases. For the fork spindles a low melting point grease, such as Castrolease Medium, Mobilgrease No. 2, Shell Retinax, Esso Grease, or Belmoline D, should be used. For the hubs use a high melting point grease such as Castrolease Heavy, Mobilgrease No. 4, Shell R.B. Grease, Esso Grease or Belmoline C.

CHAPTER VI

CARE OF ELECTRICAL EQUIPMENT

IN this chapter we are concerned solely with the electrical equipment used for lighting purposes, although in the case of the coil ignition models the battery is used both for lighting and ignition. The various components used for ignition only, such as the magneto portion of the "Magdyno," the contact breaker, coil, ignition switch and warning lamp have already been dealt with in the latter part of Chapter IV, and no further reference will be made to them here.

Where coil ignition is not used, the lighting equipment comprises (except on Model Z "Cycar" which has a Villiers set with direct lighting from a flywheel dynamo): the dynamo portion of the Lucas "Magdyno" (which is detachable); a 12 amp.-hr. battery; a Lucas type headlamp with double-filament bulb, the upper bulb giving an anti-dazzle beam controlled by a handlebar operated dimming switch; and an MT110 tail light. The lighting switch and ammeter are in the tank panel or headlamp.

On coil ignition models the lighting equipment is the same except that a Lucas type dynamo is used in conjunction with a large headlamp and MT210 tail light.

CARE OF DYNAMO (1934-6)

The Lucas " Magdyno." An excellent view of the "Magdyno" is shown in Fig. 37. As may be seen, it comprises a separate magneto and dynamo held together by means of a strap. The dynamo, with which we are alone concerned, is driven from the magneto spindle by gears and is readily detachable so that those who use "Bullet" and other fast models for racing purposes can readily strip off their lighting equipment. A suitable fitment is obtainable for protecting the gears when the dynamo portion is removed.

" Third Brush " Output Control. On the "Magdyno" what is known as the "third brush" system of regulating the dynamo output is used. This system sees to it that in spite of varying dynamo speeds the output is kept constant when running fast. Two main brushes are provided on the dynamo, one of which is earthed and the other insulated, and the third brush is provided on the underside of the commutator bracket.

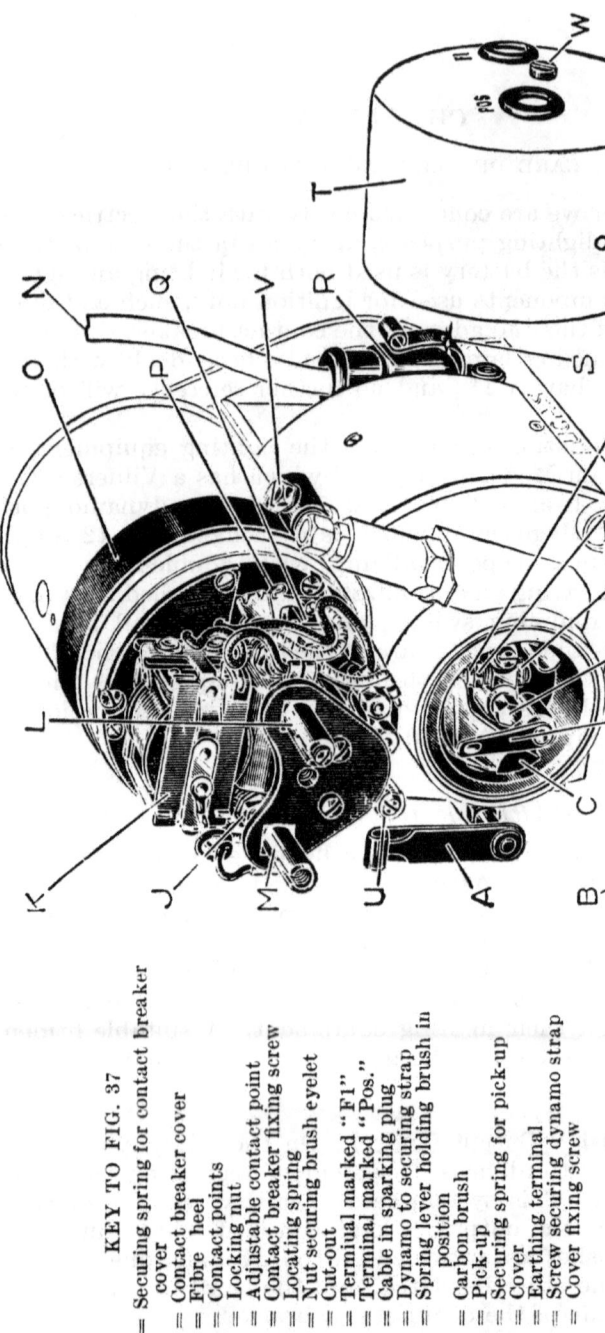

KEY TO FIG. 37

A = Securing spring for contact breaker cover
B = Contact breaker cover
C = Fibre heel
D = Contact points
E = Locking nut
F = Adjustable contact point
G = Contact breaker fixing screw
H = Locating spring
J = Nut securing brush eyelet
K = Cut-out
L = Terminal marked "F1"
M = Terminal marked "Pos."
N = Cable in sparking plug
O = Dynamo to securing strap
P = Spring lever holding brush in position
Q = Carbon brush
R = Pick-up
S = Securing spring for pick-up
T = Cover
U = Earthing terminal
V = Screw securing dynamo strap
W = Cover fixing screw

FIG. 37. THE LUCAS "MAGDYNO" WITH COVERS REMOVED (1934–6 TYPE)

CARE OF ELECTRICAL EQUIPMENT

The Cut-out. This is mounted on the dynamo end bracket and constitutes an automatic switch whose duty it is to prevent the battery discharging into the dynamo when the engine is stationary. When the voltage at the dynamo exceeds the battery voltage as the engine is accelerated, the cut-out contacts close, and when the speed is reduced and the battery voltage exceeds the dynamo voltage the contacts open, so making it absolutely impossible for the battery to discharge back through the dynamo. It should be noted, however, that the cut-out is not intended to and cannot prevent over-charging of the battery.

—Do Not Meddle with It. The cut-out is very carefully adjusted by the manufacturers, and foolish indeed is he who would meddle with it unnecessarily. Cut out any amateurish adjustments!

If by any unlucky chance the dynamo polarity becomes reversed, the remedy is to run the engine *slowly* with the switch in the "C" position and then press the cut-out contacts together momentarily.

Before Removing the Dynamo Cover. Disconnect the positive lead of the battery* to prevent the possibility of the dynamo polarity being reversed or the battery being short-circuited, either of which may cause serious damage.

A brass connector connects the lead from the positive terminal of the battery to the switch lead and to disconnect, first remove the rubber shield and then unscrew the cable connector, taking care that it does not touch any metal part of the frame. If it does touch, a spark will show that the battery has been well and truly shorted. Pull the rubber shield well over the connector when again reconnecting.

Do Commutator Brushes Make Good Contact? Occasionally remove the dynamo cover, hold the brush spring levers (*P*, Fig. 37) aside and withdraw the commutator brushes from their holders. Note whether the brushes slide freely in their holders and make good contact with the commutator. If they have been in use for a long time, they may have become so worn that they do not bed down properly on the commutator, and the only remedy is to replace the brushes by new ones of Lucas manufacture. To obtain the most satisfactory result new brushes should be "bedded" to the commutator at a Lucas service depot.

—Are They Clean? It is vitally important to keep the commutator brushes clean and after removing them they should be

---

* For safety's sake it is advisable to do this whenever any alterations to the wiring are made or whenever any of the leads are disconnected.

cleaned with a rag moistened with petrol. When refitting, see that the brushes are replaced in their correct positions. The commutator itself should also be kept clean and free from oil and carbon dust.

To Clean the Commutator. Undoubtedly the easiest and best method is without disconnecting any leads to remove one of the main brushes from its holder and insert through the aperture a fine duster held by a suitably shaped piece of wood against the commutator surface while slowly revolving the engine by hand.

The Lucas Dynamo (Coil Ignition). The Lucas E3E 6-volt dynamo used on the coil ignition models is rather similar to the dynamo portion of the "Magdyno" and employs the "third brush" system of output control and has a cut-out on the end bracket. A resistance in the dynamo field circuit sees to it that when the combined lighting and charging switch is in the "off" position it gives an output which approximately balances the current used by the ignition coil, and when the switch is moved to the "C" position or when the lamps are switched on, the dynamo gives its full output. This arrangement keeps the battery in good condition without any appreciable risk of overcharging.

Maintenance. The only periodical attention necessary is to keep the commutator and brushes clean and to see that the brushes make good contact and slide freely in their holders. On removing the dynamo cover the commutator and brushes are at once accessible and examination and cleaning may be carried out as described above for the dynamo portion of the "Magdyno."

What the Ammeter is For. This centre-zero instrument which shows a charge on one side and a discharge on the other is provided to give a reading of the amount of current flowing to and from the battery. It indicates whether or not the electrical equipment is functioning satisfactorily.

BATTERY MAINTENANCE (1934–8)

The following hints and tips on how to look after the "juice box" apply only to Lucas 12 amp.-hr. lead-acid batteries, which are fitted as standard on Royal Enfields.

Examine Acid Level Once a Month. The filler caps in the top of the battery should be removed at least once a month and the level of the acid solution inspected. The solution should just reach to the top of the plate separators (i.e. to about ¼ in. above

CARE OF ELECTRICAL EQUIPMENT

the top of the plates themselves), with the battery level. If it does not do so, top up with *distilled* water until the correct level is obtained. It is best to top up with a hydrometer.

If acid has been spilled, it must be replaced by a diluted sulphuric acid (H_2SO_4) solution of the same specific gravity as the electrolyte in the cell to which it is to be added (about 1·285).

Do not Hold a Lighted Match near the Vents. If you do, you may cause the gas escaping from the vents to ignite and "blow up" the battery. Also remember that the battery contains diluted vitroil, a devilish substance should it get in the eye.

When Laying the Equipment By. Some riders do not use their machines during some months of the year, and although the tyres will not suffer if the machine is jacked right up and kept in a dark, dry place, the battery will not tolerate being forgotten. Forgotten batteries are apt to remind one of their lonesomeness by subsequently refusing duty or failing to work efficiently. To prevent permanent sulphation of the plates when the equipment is laid by for several months, the battery should be given a small charge about once a fortnight from an independent source of electrical energy (a wireless dealer or garage will do this for a reasonable charge). Under no circumstances must the electrolyte be removed and the plates allowed to remain dry. This form of abuse causes a serious and permanent loss of capacity.

To Test Specific Gravity. If any loss of acid has occurred or the battery is misbehaving itself it is advisable to check the specific gravity with a Lucas hydrometer. The specific gravity provides a good indication of the state of charge of the battery. Readings should be taken in each cell and should be approximately the same. If one cell shows a reading differing from that of the others, probably some acid has been spilled or there may be a short between the plates. The correct S.G. figures are at a temperature of about 60 degrees Fahrenheit as follows: fully discharged, below 1·150; half discharged, 1·150–1·250; fully charged, 1·250–1·300.

New Batteries are Uncharged. On all new Royal Enfields the batteries are sent out dry and uncharged, and it is necessary to fill them with a diluted sulphuric acid solution of 1·285 S.G. and charge for 32 hours at ·8 amps. Subsequently careful dynamo charging should suffice to keep them in good condition.

LAMPS (1934–6)

The Lucas manufactured large size headlamps used on "Magdyno" and coil ignition models project powerful and most

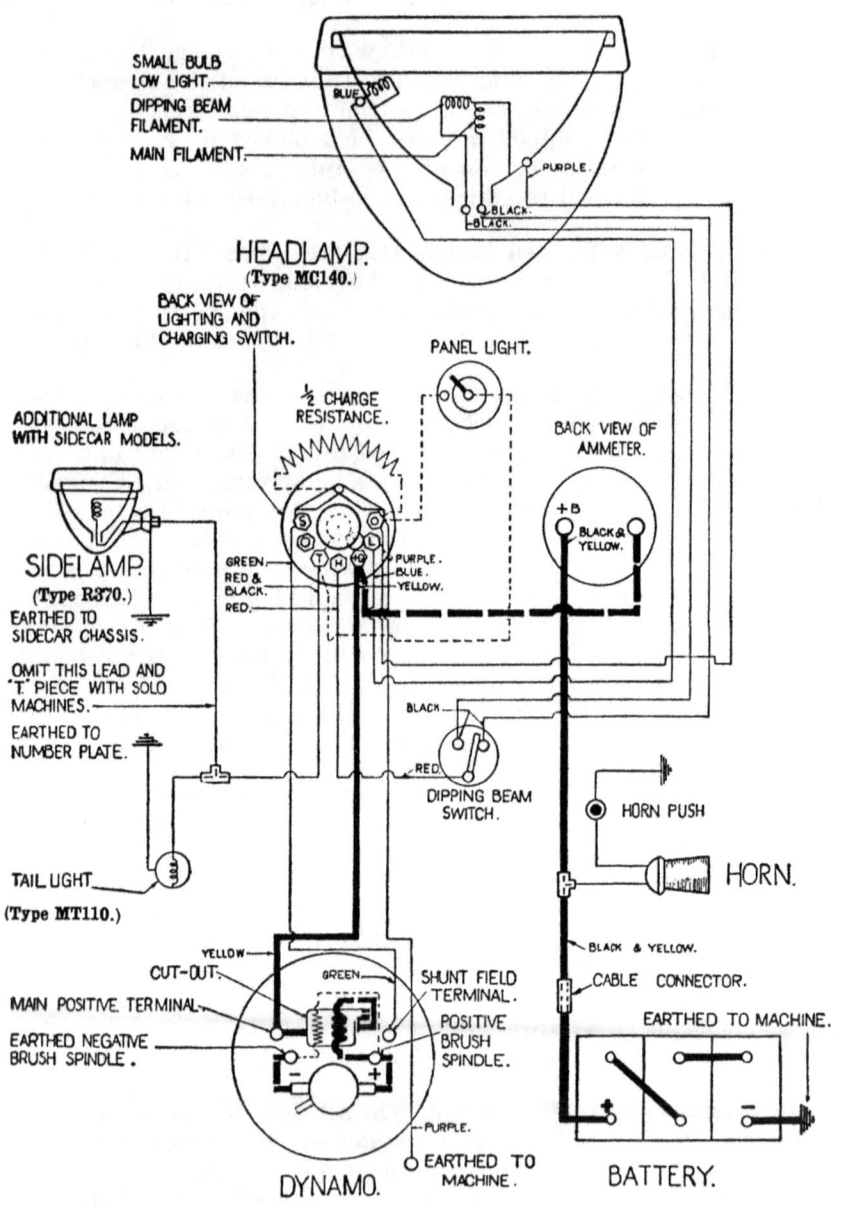

FIG. 38. WIRING DIAGRAM FOR THE LUCAS "MAGDYNO" LIGHTING EQUIPMENT WITHOUT AUTOMATIC VOLTAGE CONTROL
A W.D. for the E3E dynamo and coil equipment will be found on page 77.

CARE OF ELECTRICAL EQUIPMENT

effective beams of light if the battery is kept well charged, the lamps properly focused and the reflectors clean.

Headlamp Details. Both types of headlamp have double filament bulbs. One filament is arranged to be slightly above the other one and out of focus, and this provides the dipped, anti-dazzling beam brought into use by the handlebar switch (Fig. 7)

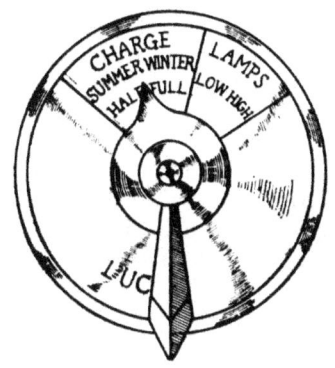 

Fig. 39. Showing Headlamp Switch Positions (1934–6)
On the right are shown the switch positions on the "Magdyno" models and on the left the positions on the coil ignition models.

when encountering oncoming traffic or when driving in misty or foggy conditions. The second filament, which is arranged just below the dipping beam filament at approximately the reflector focus, is responsible for the main normal driving beam. A small pilot bulb is also included to save current when parking the machine and for use when driving in well illuminated districts.

Switch Positions ("Magdyno" Models). The switch (see Fig. 39) which is mounted on the instrument panel along with the ammeter has the following four positions—
 "Off"—Lamps off and dynamo not charging.
 "C"—Lamps off and dynamo giving half its normal output.
 "H"—Headlamp (main bulb), tail light and sidecar light (where fitted) on; dynamo delivering full output.
 "L"—Except that the pilot bulb is in use, the conditions are the same as for the "H" position.

The dynamo output is controlled by inserting a resistance into the field circuit which is cut out automatically when the lamps are switched on.

Switch Positions (Coil Ignition Models). The switch (see Fig. 39) which is situated behind the ammeter on the tank panel and has a

detachable ignition key in the centre (see page 15), provides four positions, which are as follows—
"Summer Half Charge"—Lamps off and dynamo charging at half its full output.
"Winter Half Charge"—Lamps off and dynamo charging at full output.
"High"—All lamps on and dynamo charging at full output.
"Low"—Pilot light and tail light on.
When the switch is in the "High" position the double-filament bulb can be dipped by the finger-operated handlebar switch. The switch itself (apart from the ignition key) is completely independent of the ignition.

Battery Charging ("Magdyno" Models). Hard and fast rules obviously cannot be laid down owing to the varying conditions of riding and the time during which the machine is ridden after dark. As a rough guide, however, it may be mentioned that during the summer the switch should be left in the "C" position for about one hour daily. If the night work is considerable or the battery is in a low state of charge (S.G. 1·210 or below), increase the charging period. Never leave the battery fully discharged.

Battery Charging (Coil Ignition Models). The switch provides two alternative rates of charge. The "Summer Half Charge" position provides ample current for the coil plus a small reserve at normal speeds. When the battery is known to be already well charged this position should be used. The "Winter Full Charge" position gives the maximum dynamo output and should be employed mainly when driving at low speeds (i.e. in congested traffic) and also during the first hour or so of a long run if the battery is known to be run down. Do not run continually with the switch giving the full charging rate, otherwise you may damage the battery.

Correct Bulb Replacements. Bulbs do not last for ever and carelessness is responsible for a good many "going west" prematurely. When a bulb does go, see that a Lucas bulb of the correct type is fitted. With the Lucas type headlamp ("Magdyno") fit a Lucas No. 70, 6-volt, 24 watt double-filament gas-filled driving and dipped beam bulb and a No. 200 3 watt centre-contact bulb for the pilot, tail and sidecar lamp where fitted.

With the Lucas headlamp (coil) fit a 6-volt, 18 watt (3 amp.) double-filament bulb and a 6-volt 3 watt (·5 amp.) bulb for the pilot and tail light. In the case of the warning light (see page 49), on some models the light goes out as the engine is accelerated, but on others it does not do so. In the former case fit a 3·5-volt

CARE OF ELECTRICAL EQUIPMENT

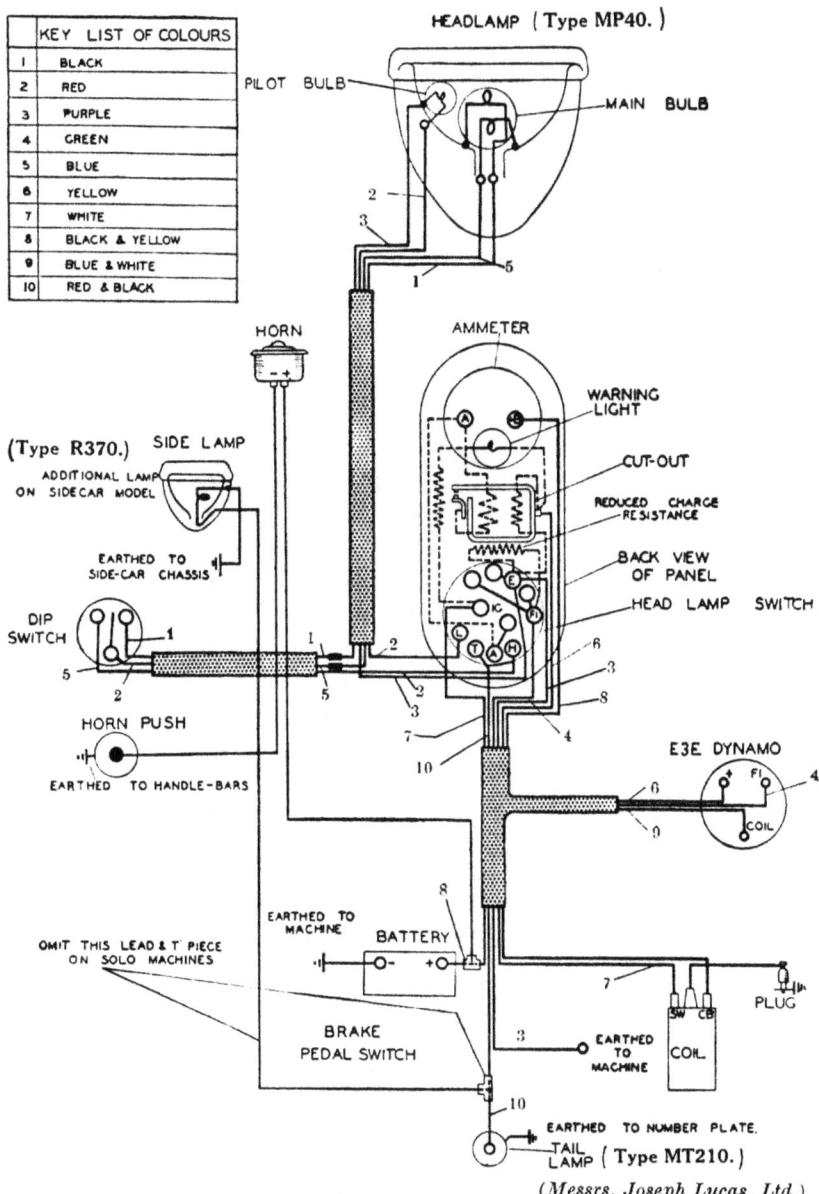

Fig. 40. Wiring Diagram for the Dynamo Lighting and Coil Ignition Equipment without Automatic Voltage Control A W.D. for the "Magdyno" lighting equipment will be found on page 74.

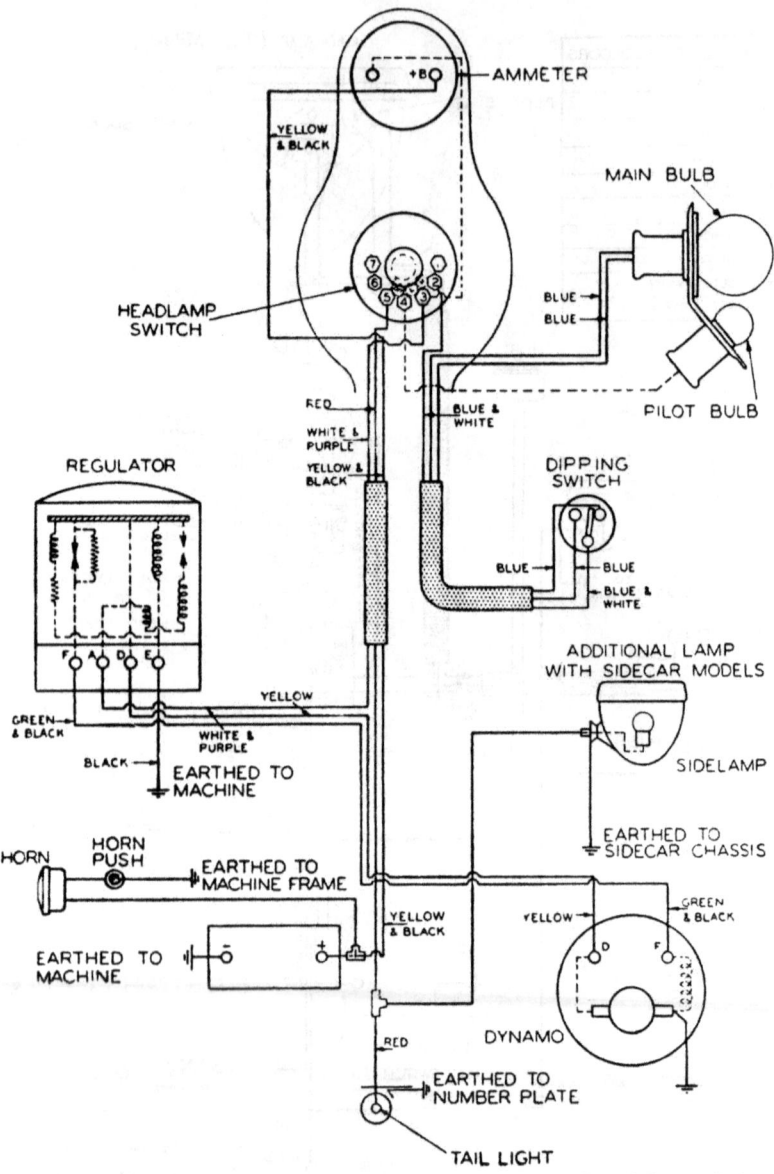

(*Joseph Lucas, Ltd.*)

Fig. 41. Wiring Diagram for "Magdyno" Lighting Equipment with Automatic Voltage Control (1938 Models without Instrument Panel)

All internal connexions are shown dotted and the cable ends are identified by coloured sleevings.

CARE OF ELECTRICAL EQUIPMENT

·3 amp. bulb and in the latter case a 2·5-volt ·2 amp. bulb. If bulbs of lower amperage are used they will rapidly burn out.

On the Villiers headlamp used on Model Z "Cycar," fit a 6 volt 1 amp. main bulb and a 6-volt ·5 amp. dimming bulb. For the tail light use either a 6-volt ·5 amp. bulb or a 6-volt ·3 amp. bulb. The latter bulb gives somewhat greater brilliance, but is apt to burn out rather quickly.

Fitting Bulbs and Focusing. On all Lucas lamps it is a very simple matter to fit new bulbs, and instructions for doing this are given hereafter. After fitting a new headlamp bulb care should be taken to see that it is correctly focused, otherwise the maximum illuminating power will not be obtained.

Headlamp ("Magdyno"). To remove the front of this lamp, all that is necessary is to slacken the fixing screw and then lift the front off. To focus the lamp, withdraw from its three supports the reflector and then slacken the clamping clip on the bulb holder at the rear of the reflector. The bulb holder can then be moved forwards or backwards until the correct focus is obtained. Afterwards tighten the clamping clip so as to lock the adjustment.

Headlamp (Coil "R.E's"). In order to replace a bulb slacken the fixing screw and withdraw the front and reflector. To remove the bulb holder, press down the ends of the retaining springs and withdraw them from the slots in which they locate. To focus the main bulb, with the front and reflector removed, slacken the clamping screw fixing the bulb holder and move both the bulb and holder until correct focus is obtained. Afterwards tighten the clamping screw.

Lucas Tail Light ("Magdyno"). To detach the rear portion of the lamp for bulb replacement, give it a half turn to the left, when it becomes detached from its fixing.

Lucas Tail Light (Coil). The rear part of this lamp can be detached for bulb replacement by depressing the spring catches provided.

Lucas Sidecar Lamp. Slacken the fixing screw to remove the front and reflector. For bulb replacement, withdraw the bulb holder from the back of the reflector. Alternative positions for the bulb are provided and each should be experimented with until the best result is obtained.

Keep the Reflectors Clean. Wipe over chromium-plated surfaces with a damp cloth to remove dirt or dust and polish ebony

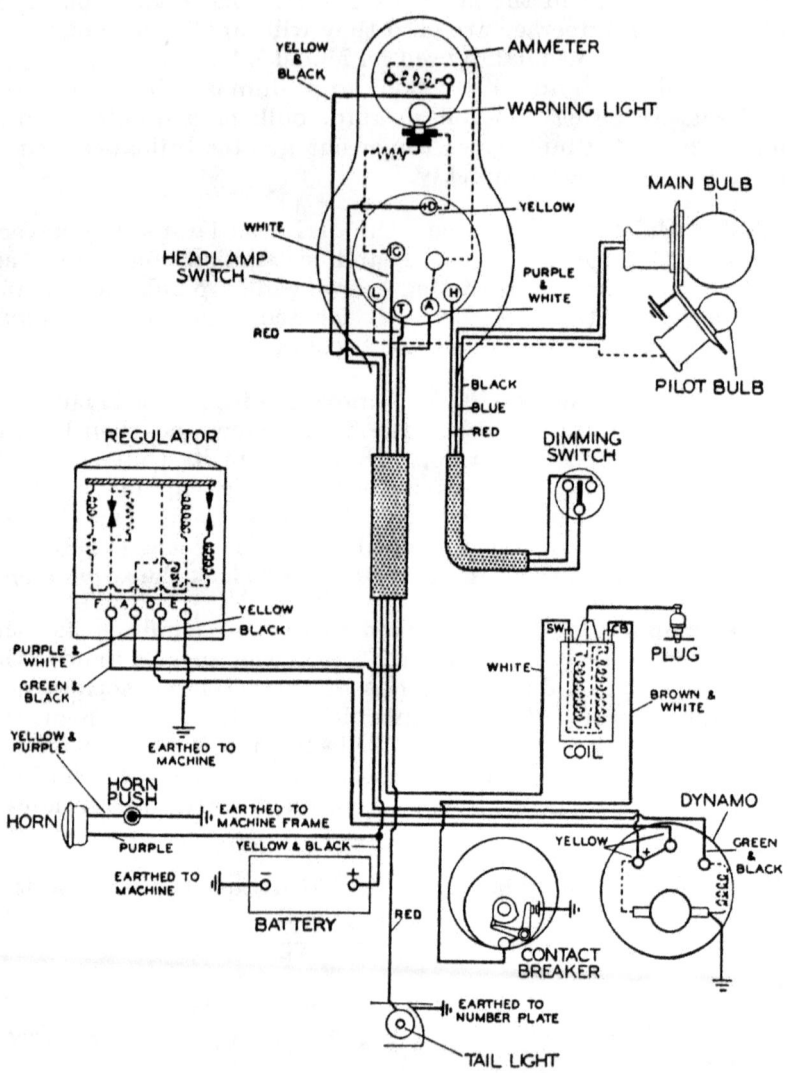

(*Messrs. Joseph Lucas, Ltd.*)

Fig. 42. Wiring Diagram for the Dynamo Lighting and Coil Ignition Equipment with Automatic Voltage Control

This diagram is applicable to all 1938 coil ignition models. On the 1937 models a tank panel housing the ammeter and lighting switch was provided. All internal connexions are shown dotted.

CARE OF ELECTRICAL EQUIPMENT

black surfaces with a good furniture or car polish. Metal polish is taboo. Lightly polish with a soft cloth or chamois leather the transparent reflector covering.

Examine the Wiring Occasionally. See that none of the wires have become chafed or disconnected, particularly the battery leads and the positive lead from the dynamo to the switch panel. Should the dynamo go on strike, possibly it may be due to a faulty lead. As a makeshift measure, disconnect the field circuit lead (green marking) from the dynamo. This will not cause the dynamo to charge, but it will prevent it from being damaged.

CARE OF DYNAMO (1937-8)

All 1937-8 Royal Enfield four-stroke models incorporate automatic voltage control in the "Magdyno" or coil ignition and lighting equipment. The dynamo portion of the "Magdyno" or the dynamo (coil) is very similar to the earlier Lucas types, but the "third brush" is omitted since the automatic voltage control device entirely regulates the dynamo output. The cut-out has also been eliminated, this now being combined with the voltage control unit. The ignition portion of the new "Magdyno" has already been referred to on page 46.

Dynamo Maintenance. The advice given on pages 69-72 holds good for 1937-8 dynamos with the exception, of course, of the paragraphs dealing with the "third brush" and the cut-out which are no longer applicable. A sketch showing the commutator end of the 1937-8 dynamo is included on page 82, and it will be noticed that a lubricator is provided on the commutator end bracket. A few drops of thin machine oil should be inserted here about every 4000-5000 miles. The driving end bearing is packed with grease on assembly and this should suffice until it is necessary to strip-down the motor-cycle for a general overhaul, when the dynamo should be returned to the nearest Lucas Service Depot for cleaning, repacking with grease, and adjustment.

Do Not Tamper with Automatic Voltage Control Unit. This ingenious device, comprising the cut-out and automatic voltage control neatly housed in a box separate from the dynamo, sees to it that the battery is always kept properly charged by varying the dynamo output according to the load and state of charge of the battery. When the battery is run down, the dynamo gives a big output to recharge it as quickly as possible. The regulator effects an increased output when the lights are switched on, so as to balance the current consumed by them. The unit is sealed and should not be tampered with, the only likely trouble, and a remote one, being oxidization, or possibly welding together, of the points due to accidental crossing of the dynamo field and positive leads. Therefore be careful with the leads at the dynamo end. See also notes on page 50 *re* running with battery disconnected.

The automatic voltage control prevents boiling away of the

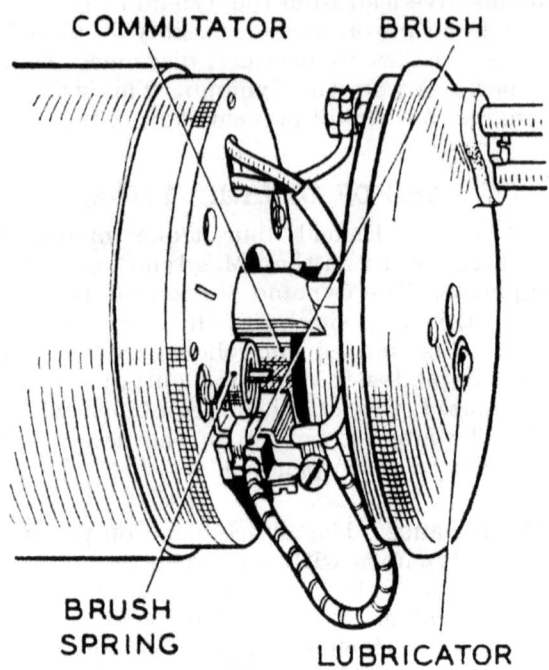

Fig. 43. Commutator End of 1937-8 Lucas Dynamo

distilled water in the battery because with the battery well charged the dynamo gives only a trickle charge (1 or 2 amperes at the ammeter) during daylight running. Nevertheless the level and S.G. of the electrolyte should occasionally be checked. Follow the hints given on pages 72-73. If a "Lucas-Nife" battery is substituted for the lead-acid type a new regulator should be fitted, otherwise the dynamo charging rate with a run down battery will be reduced.

Examine Wiring Occasionally. The various leads in the wiring system should be examined occasionally for chafing or bad contact at the terminals. This is particularly important in the case of the two battery leads and the leads from the voltage control unit to the dynamo and earth. Should the dynamo cease to charge

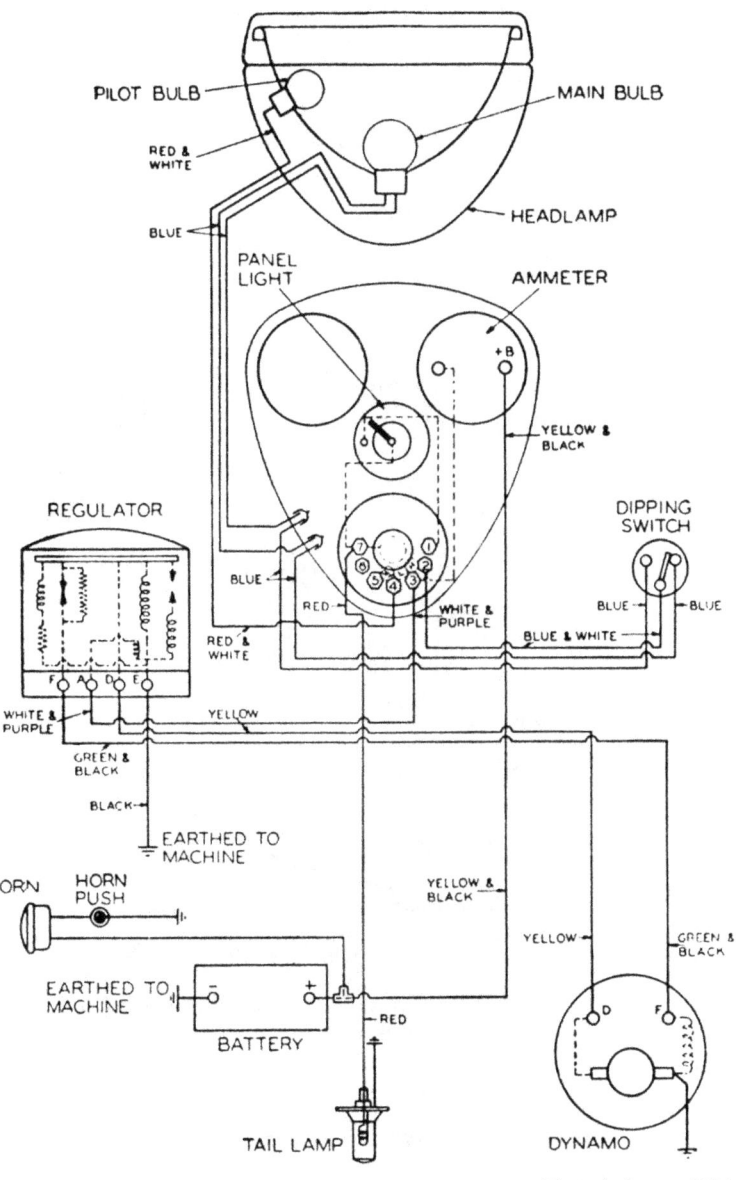

Fig. 44. Wiring Diagram for "Magdyno" Lighting Equipment with Automatic Voltage Control (1937 Models with Instrument Panel)

All internal connexions are shown dotted and the cable ends are identified by coloured sleevings.

84   BOOK OF THE ROYAL ENFIELD

(indicated by a heavy discharge at the ammeter), disconnect the field circuit lead (marked green) from the dynamo; this may save the dynamo from damage, though it will not cause it to charge.

LAMPS (1937-8)

As on the 1934-6 models, Lucas lamps are fitted, the headlamp having a double-filament main bulb, the out-of-focus bulb being

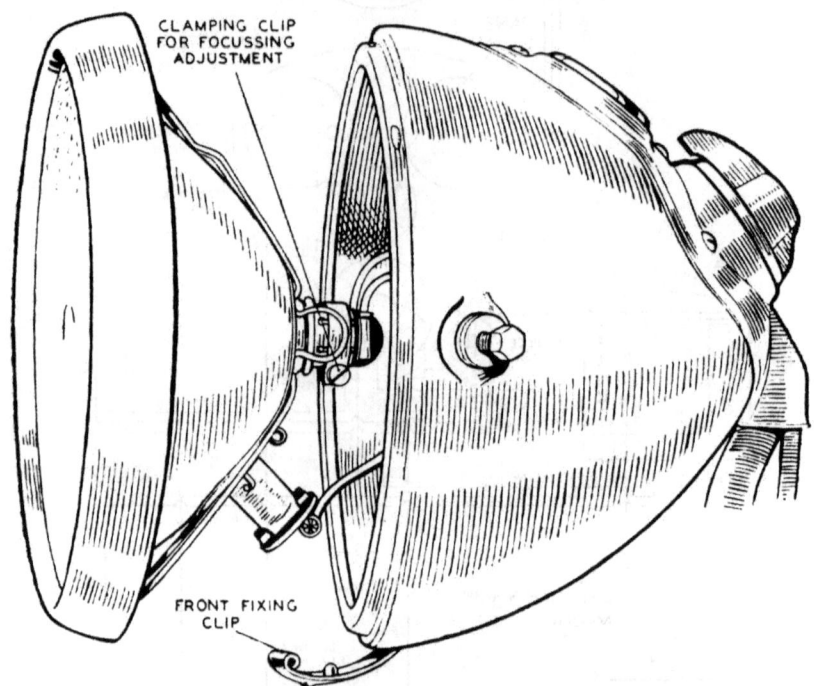

FIG. 45. THE LUCAS HEADLAMP USED ON 1938 MODELS

controlled by a handlebar dip switch. A pilot bulb is, of course, also included. On 1937 models the ammeter and lighting switch are mounted on the instrument panel, but on all 1938 models they are embodied in the headlamp.

Switch Positions ("**Magdyno**" **Models**). The lighting switch which is mounted on the instrument panel or else on the headlamp behind the ammeter (Fig. 45) without the inclusion of a half-charge resistance as hitherto, has the following three positions—

"Off"—Lamps off.

"L"—Headlamp (pilot bulb) tail light and sidecar light (where fitted).

CARE OF ELECTRICAL EQUIPMENT

"H"—Headlamp (main bulb), tail light and sidecar light (where fitted).

It should be noted that the dynamo *in all switch positions* charges according to the load on the battery and its state of charge.

Switch Positions (Coil Ignition Models). The switch on the tank panel (1937) or headlamp (1938) has the same positions as on the "Magdyno" models, but instead of being marked "Off," "L," "H" they are marked "Off," "Low," and "High." In the centre of the switch is the ignition key and a warning lamp (see page 49) is included.

Correct Bulb Replacements. For all 1937–8 lamps use the correct bulb replacements as recommended on page 76. To assist in identification, Lucas bulbs are marked on the metal cap with a number. Be careful to fit the double-filament bulb with the dipped beam filament *above* the centre filament. Bulbs should be replaced before they are burnt out, as it is impossible to focus them correctly when the filaments sag.

Focusing Headlamps. To remove the lamp front, press back the fixing clip at the bottom of the lamp. When replacing, locate the top of the rim first. To remove the bulb holder, press back the two securing springs. The main bulb can be focussed by removing the lamp front and reflector and slackening the clamping screw securing the bulb holder. Move the bulb and holder until a long range beam without any dark centre is obtained. Finally retighten the clamping screw.

Cleaning Reflectors. Deal with these as described on page 79.

CHAPTER VII

ADJUSTMENTS AND OVERHAULING

IN this chapter the author has aimed at putting in a convenient form all the information and data necessary to enable the Enfield owner to keep his machine and engine in first-class trim, and this it is hoped will be of value both to novices and experts. All motorcycles, and for that matter all mechanical contrivances, require

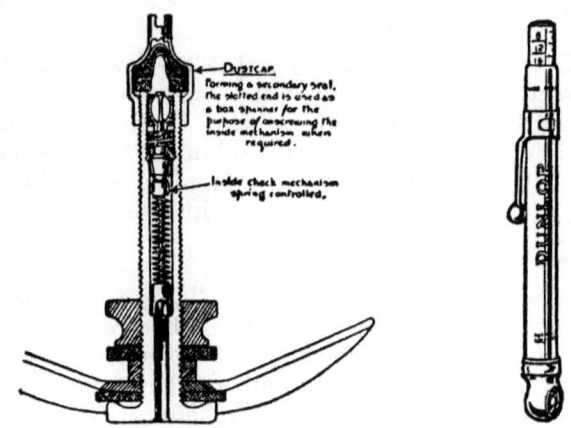

FIGS. 46, 47. SHOWING (*Left*) DUNLOP VALVE AND (*Right*) POCKET PRESSURE GAUGE

periodic lubrication, minor adjustments, and occasional overhauling; and at regular intervals the I.C. engine requires to be decarbonized and the valves ground-in if a reasonable degree of efficiency is to be maintained. The tyres must also be looked after.

HOW TO OBTAIN GOOD TYRE MILEAGE

The Dunlop cord tyres fitted as standard on all Royal Enfield models are made of the very finest material by a firm which has the world's land speed record to its credit, and with proper attention these tyres will give a very big trouble-free mileage. To obtain the best result from your tyres you should—

Always Maintain Correct Tyre Pressures. All Dunlop tyres are now fitted with Schrader valves and, with the aid of a pressure

ADJUSTMENTS AND OVERHAULING 87

gauge, the pressure can be measured accurately. The author recommends the Dunlop Pencil Type No. 1 gauge, illustrated in Fig. 47. This gauge is extremely convenient as it has a clip to fit the waistcoat pocket. To use this gauge, the valve dust cap (Fig. 46) is taken off, and the end of the pressure gauge is pressed on to the open end of the valve. It depresses the pin and allows

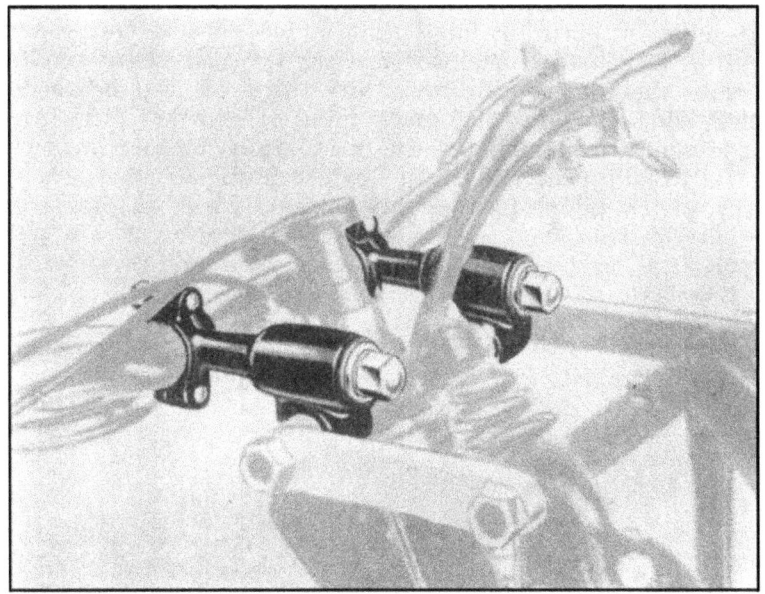

FIG. 48. TO PREVENT RIDING FATIGUE—THE RUBBER MOUNTED HANDLEBARS

On all the larger 1938 models a new design of rubber mounted handlebars is provided. This makes riding much less tiring as it absorbs all road shocks and engine vibration. The Royal Enfield handlebars, unlike some insulated types, are adjustable for angle as well as height. It pays to find the most suitable position for individual requirements.

air to enter the gauge and push up the piston calibrated in pounds per square inch. It is always wise to keep the dust caps screwed on, though some riders throw them away! Dust or grit getting into the valve stem is liable to interfere with the valve action of the little spring-controlled plunger (Fig. 46) and cause leakage. About once a year valve "insides" (1s. per box of five) should be replaced. They can be removed by taking off the valve cap and using the slotted end as a screwdriver.

If desired what are known as "Duplchek" valve caps can be fitted in place of the standard caps and these besides protecting the main valve, form a secondary seal against air leakage and enable the pressure gauge to be applied without removing them.

The recommended inflation pressures for the Dunlop cord tyres (standard size) fitted on the 1936-8 Royal Enfields are tabulated below, and you should observe them as far as possible. About once a week, certainly not less than once a fortnight, test the pressures in the tyres with the pressure gauge and pump up until the gauge registers the correct pressures.

It must be borne in mind that under-inflation causes severe strain to be set up in the casing of the tyre. If run at too low a pressure the casings will crack and the tyres will be rendered useless when there are still many miles of wear left in the tread. The pressures recommended are, incidentally, for machines which are fully equipped, and if the driver and passenger are very heavy, or if a pillion passenger is habitually carried, higher pressure in the rear tyre, at any rate, is advisable. For a pillion passenger at least an extra 5 lb. per sq. in. should be allowed for the rear tyre.

INFLATION PRESSURES FOR 1936-8 MODELS

Model	Front	Rear	Sidecar
A, T, TM (solo)	16	24	—
B, BM, C, CM, CO, S, SM, S2 (solo)	18	26	—
G, J, JM, H, HM (solo)	16	22	—
G, J, JM, H, HM (sidecar)	20	24	16
L, 500 "Bullet" J2 (solo)	16	18	—
L, 500 "Bullet" J2 (sidecar)	20	20	16
250, 350 "Bullet" (solo)	18	22	—
500 Competition	18	16	—
K, KX (solo)	16	18	—
K, KX (single-seater sidecar)	16	22	16

Examine the Tyres Occasionally. If you wish to cut down the risk of roadside hold-ups to the minimum and avoid preventable deterioration of the covers, you should occasionally jack the machine up and carefully examine the treads over the whole of their circumference. Any sharp little flints embedded in the rubber should be gently eased out with a pocket knife and if the flints are of appreciable size, the holes should afterwards be stopped. In time it is inevitable that the tyres will become cut by the glass and sharp flints which are to be found on all our roads. A superficial cut in the rubber is of little account, but it may spread, and it should therefore be filled with a suitable tyre stopping. If, however, this cut extends to the fabric of the tyre, wet will penetrate into the latter and, in due course, will rot it. Any cut of this nature should therefore be repaired

ADJUSTMENTS AND OVERHAULING

efficiently. The only way to get this done is to remove the tyre and have it vulcanized. Vulcanizing is now much cheaper than it used to be.

Things You Should Avoid. Freak hills and extremely rough surfaces should be avoided. Wheel spin in particular is extremely detrimental to the rear tyre. The majority of riders never subject their tyres to these exceptional conditions, but many of them do not appreciate the strain which they impose on their tyres by bad driving. Fierce braking, rapid acceleration and fast cornering (particularly on a sidecar machine) should be avoided as far as possible, the same applying to quick engagement of the clutch with a wide throttle opening. This latter procedure, incidentally, is also detrimental to the transmission system. Three important points not yet mentioned are:
(a) avoid crossing upraised tram lines or running in the lines;
(b) do not allow the tyres to stand in patches of oil or paraffin;
(c) when pulling up by the kerb do not allow the side of the tyre to scrape it.

Do You Know This? In recent years tyres became so well-made and reliable that it was customary for many riders to get the last pennyworth out of their tyres by riding until the fabric almost showed through (fast riders, of course, would never do this). This practice now invites trouble—for it is actually illegal to-day to run with smooth tyres (i.e. when all effective tread has disappeared), and it is better to buy a new cover than to waste the money on a fine.

How to Remove a Tyre Without Struggling with it. It is a frequent sight for the author to see a motor-cyclist *struggling* to remove a tyre, and through faulty refitting the tube is sometimes pinched and a second repair becomes necessary. Tyre removal and replacement need offer no difficulty whatever if a few simple precautions are taken. All Enfield motor-cycles are now fitted with Dunlop cord tyres, which have inextensible wired edges fitting into well-base rims. To remove this type of tyre, first completely deflate it by removing all the valve parts, including the check mechanism (Fig. 46). Then, at a point opposite the valve, push the edges of the cover into the well-base rim. Proceed to remove the tyre edge as shown in Fig. 49, by inserting two small levers, one each side of the valve about 4 in. apart. No force should be necessary *as long as the edges of the tyre opposite the valve are right down in the rim*. Gradually work round until the whole of the tyre edge comes off the rim, enabling the tube to be withdrawn. Do not employ large tyre levers. The detachable mudguard and on some machines the knock-out rear spindle (pages 4 and 102) greatly simplifies repairs.

Refitting Same. Assuming one edge of the tyre is already in position, slightly inflate the inner tube, insert it inside the cover, and push the valve stem through the hole in the rim. Do not tighten up the lock-nut securing the valve to the rim, and also see that the tube is not twisted. Then start to fit the second edge of the cover at a point diametrically opposite the valve, by placing it over the rim and pushing it down into the rim base. Push on the rest of the cover and, with a pair of small tyre levers, work round each side in such a way that the part near the valve is refitted last. On no account use excessive force, and while inflating see that the edges of the cover bed down evenly on the rim. Finally, replace the valve lock-nut and pump up the tyre to the recommended pressure. After a puncture has been repaired do not immediately pump up to full pressure, but give the patch a chance to stick on hard. In connection with punctures, the following two points are important: (*a*) See that the solution is "tacky" before applying the patch, (*b*) don't be stingy with the french chalk.

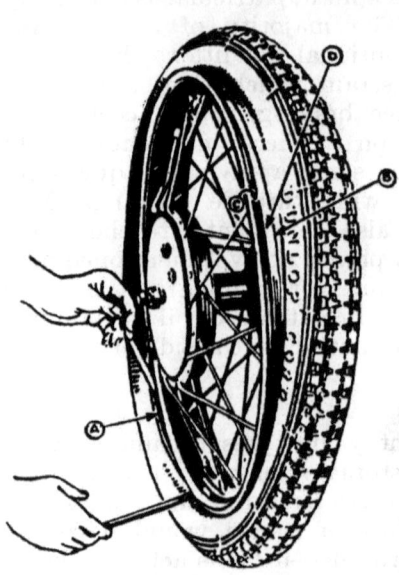

FIG. 49. HOW TO REMOVE A FRONT COVER

The tyre edges at *A* cannot be levered off until the edges at *B* are first pushed down into the well-base rim *D* off the rim *C*.

Keep Wheels In Alignment. Rapid tyre wear can often be traced to bad alignment of the wheels and when retensioning the secondary chain (see page 100) you should be careful to adjust the set pins in the rear fork ends an equal amount either side. Should an examination of the tyre treads reveal uneven wear or should you suspect misalignment of the wheels check the alignment on a solo model with the assistance of a straight piece of wood and on a sidecar machine with two similar pieces of wood.

It is, of course, absolutely essential that the edge of the board should be dead straight and square, and that it should be at least

ADJUSTMENTS AND OVERHAULING

as long as the machine itself. Let us take the case of the solo motor-cycle first. Put the machine on the stand and place the straight edge of the board alongside the two wheels, as high up as possible. Then turn the front wheel until the board touches both sides of the front tyre and at least one side of the rear tyre. If the wheels are in line the board should also touch both sides of the rear wheel tyre; if it does not do so the alignment of the rear

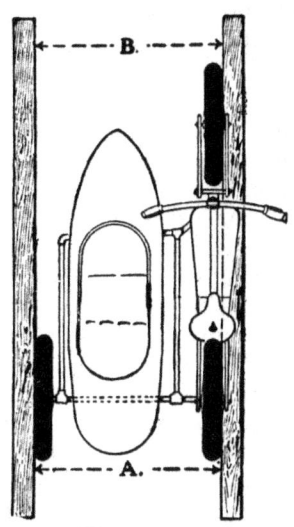

FIG. 50. CHECKING WHEEL AND SIDECAR ALIGNMENT BY MEANS OF BOARDS PLACED ALONG THE EDGES OF THE WHEELS

wheel must be altered by means of the fork set pins. If correct alignment cannot be obtained it is probable that the frame or forks are twisted.

Alignment of a Sidecar Machine. When lining up a sidecar the two wheels of the machine itself must first be checked in the manner described above. The board must then be set along the offside of the tyres and a similar board placed across the sidecar tyre as shown in Fig. 50. The distances between the boards at A and B must then be measured. In theory these distances should be equal, but, in practice, it is found that better steering is obtained if B is about $\frac{1}{4}$ in. less than A. Wheel alignment is obtained by sliding the drop arm from the rear ball joint along the sidecar frame tube. Finally check that the motor-cycle is quite vertical or leaning towards the sidecar slightly (most riders prefer this) and make the necessary adjustment to the sidecar connexions if required.

ROUTINE ADJUSTMENTS

There are a number of minor adjustments which it is desirable that the Enfield rider should attend to every few hundred miles, or when circumstances necessitate these adjustments being made. If the rider values his machine, however, he will not wait till adjustment *has* to be made, but will carefully inspect his machine as a matter of routine and make the necessary adjustments before they become absolutely essential. By doing this much time and money is in the long run saved, and the performance of the machine will be kept at its maximum.

Cleaning. It requires a considerable amount of time to keep a motor-cycle in anything approaching "showroom" condition, but it is the author's opinion that, unless a machine be kept reasonably clean, the fullest pleasure and maximum efficiency cannot be obtained from it. Apart from the question of pride of ownership (and the present range is very handsome indeed with the enamel and chromium plating unsoiled), it is an undoubted fact that dirt covers a multitude of defects and greatly accelerates depreciation in respect of market value. This is, of course, obvious. If neglected, a motor-cycle rapidly becomes shabby and an eyesore. After a ride in dirty weather, cleaning may take at least an hour. It entails the use of stiff bristle brushes and paraffin for removing the filth from the lower extremities, together with cloths, leather, and polish for the enamelled parts. On no account should a machine be left soaking wet overnight. A serious amount of rusting may ensue. If the rider is so preoccupied that he cannot spare the necessary time for cleaning, the machine should be thoroughly greased all over before use.

Wash fabric-covered sidecars with soap and lukewarm water, or if very dirty clean first with paraffin. Sidecar upholstery and windscreen aprons should be wiped over with a damp cloth and polished with furniture cream. Use metal polish such as "Brasso" for cleaning celluloid.

It should be noted that chromium plating does not require and should not be treated with metal polish, for it does not oxidize in the same manner as nickel plating. The chromium-plated parts should be treated similarly to the enamel, and the surfaces will then improve with cleaning.

Lubrication. This is comprehensively dealt with in Chapter V and no further reference is made in this chapter.

Adjustments to Carburettor and Ignition System. These are fully dealt with in Chapter IV.

ADJUSTMENTS AND OVERHAULING 93

For the Sake of the Valves, Maintain Correct Clearances. The exhaust valve operates in a place where the temperature is often in the region of 1000 degrees Centigrade. Just imagine what the valve face and its seat are subjected to if the valve fails to close completely during the firing stroke! Unless a sufficient clearance exists when the engine is running between the end of the valve stem and its tappet, rocker or rocker screw, there is a grave danger of the exhaust valve burning, distorting, or even fracturing. If the latter happens on an O.H.V. engine a well-wrecked engine may be thrown into the bargain. Insufficient clearances at the inlet and exhaust valves also cause considerable loss of compression and power and general efficiency. Excessive clearances create valve clatter and also put excessive strain on the valves.

How to Check Them. On all Royal Enfield four-stroke engines the valve clearances should occasionally be checked with a feeler gauge (except in the case of some O.H.V. engines where no inlet clearance is recommended) and if necessary adjusted as described below. In the case of *new* engines, owing to the initial bedding down of the contacting surfaces, the valve clearances should be checked and if necessary adjusted after the first 500 miles running. Subsequently they require attention at less frequent intervals. Usually the expert rider can tell instinctively by the "feel" and exhaust note of his engine whether the valve clearances are O.K. To obtain access to the tappets or rockers as the case may be, it is only necessary to remove the quickly-detachable cover which encloses them (not provided on Model LF).

RECOMMENDED VALVE CLEARANCES ON 1934–5 ENGINES. (See also page 121).

Model	Inlet Valve (s)	Exhaust Valve
S.V. (B, C, L, K) . .	·004 inches	·006 inches
O.H.V. (BO, G, LF) . .	No clearance	·002 inches
O.H.V. (LO, LO2, S, S2, T) .	No clearance	·005 inches

On all 1934–8 Royal Enfields the valve clearances should be checked with the piston on top of the compression stroke and the engine *cold*, and a feeler gauge of the correct thickness (see table) should just slide without binding between the end of the valve stem and the adjustable tappet head on the side-valve engines, and between the end of the valve stem and the overhead rocker or rocker screw in the case of the overhead-valve engines. Where no clearance is recommended for the inlet valve(s) on the O.H.V. engines, the adjustment should be such that the rockers or tappets can just be moved endways without any perceptible up and down play. Where adjustable rocker screws are provided it should be possible to pass a single thickness of tissue paper between the end of the adjusting screw and the valve stem. Before checking the exhaust valve clearance, see that the exhaust valve lifter (page 96) is adjusted correctly and is not keeping the valve off its seat. See page 121 for 1936-8.

Tappet Adjustment (1934-8 S.V. Models B, C, L, H. K). After removing the valve

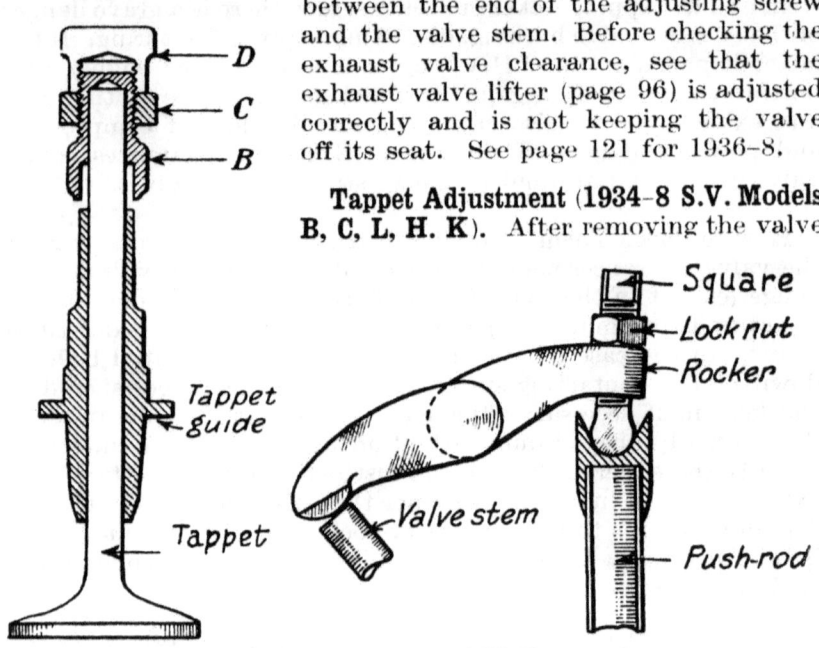

FIG. 51. S.V. TAPPET ADJUSTMENT (All 1934-8 S.V. Models)

FIG. 52. O.H. ROCKER ADJUSTMENT (1934-5 MODELS BO, G, S, S2, T)

spring cover (two on Model K) and putting the piston at the top of the compression stroke, deal with each flatbase tappet as follows—

Referring to Fig. 51 which shows a tappet and its guide, hold the tappet with a spanner applied to the lock-nut *C* (middle hexagon) and apply another spanner to the adjustable tappet head *D* (top hexagon). Then unlock the head by turning it to the right and the lock-nut to the left. The tappet clearance can then be adjusted (see table on page 93) by holding the bottom hexagon *B* on the tappet itself with one spanner and then rotating the head and lock-nut up or down so as to lengthen or shorten the tappet as required. See that the lock-nut is securely retightened and check the valve clearance afterwards in case the tappet head has shifted.

ADJUSTMENTS AND OVERHAULING

O.H. Rocker Adjustment (1934-5 Models BO, G, S, S2, T). On these five engines the valve clearances are adjusted by means of the ball-ended adjuster screws at the push-rod ends of the rockers (see Fig. 52). To make an adjustment, all that is necessary is to remove the rocker inspection cover, hold with a spanner the upper squared end of the adjuster screw, slacken the lock-nut

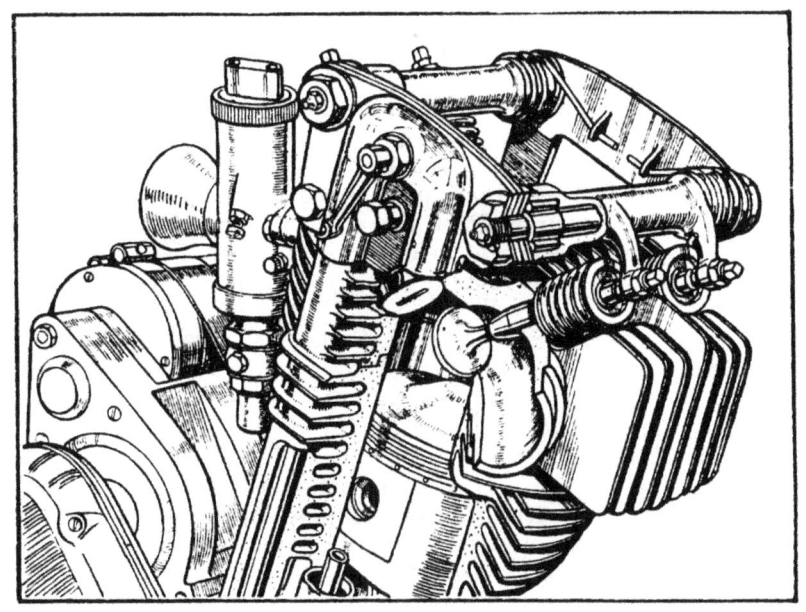

(*From "The Motor Cycle"*)

Fig. 53. O.H. Rocker Adjustment (1934 Model LF)

and then turn the adjuster screw to the left or right until the correct valve clearance (see page 93) is obtained.

O.H. Rocker Adjustment (1934 O.H.V. Model LF). On this four-valve engine (replaced by the '35 three-valve engine) the four overhead rockers each have a separate adjustment for the valve clearances, but whereas two-valve engines have 1934-5 adjusting screws situated at the push-rod ends of the rockers, the four-valve engine has the square-ended adjuster screws provided at the valve ends of the rockers. The arrangement is clearly shown in Fig. 53. The adjustment itself is made in exactly the same way as on the two-valve engines (see preceding paragraph), the lock-nut being unscrewed and a spanner applied to the squared end until the correct valve clearance (page 93) is obtained. On the LF engine the overhead valve gear is not enclosed as on the other engines.

Push-rod Adjustment (1935 Models LO, LO2). The two '35 three-valve engines, which are of identical design, have no overhead rocker adjustment for correcting the valve clearances as on the other O.H.V. engines, but instead have an adjustment at the foot of each push-rod. This may be understood from the excellent sectional view of the three-valve engine reproduced by kind permission of *The Motor Cycle* in Fig. 54. To adjust the valve clearances (checked at the overhead rockers, of course) it is only necessary to remove the plated cover at the cylinder base and then shorten or lengthen each push-rod the amount required to give the correct clearance (page 93) by loosening the lock-nut and then screwing up or down the screwed ball end of the pushrod. Finally tighten the lock-nut securely, check the clearances and replace the covers. For 1937–8 adjustment, see page 121.

Always Maintain Backlash at Exhaust Valve Lifter. It is important before checking the valve clearances and at all other times always to maintain a small amount ($\frac{1}{16}$ in. to $\frac{1}{8}$ in.) of backlash at the exhaust valve lifter lever with the exhaust valve fully closed, otherwise it is quite impossible for the valve to seat properly and loss of compression, power and burning of the valve (see page 93) will inevitably be occasioned, accompanied probably by a considerable amount of banging in the exhaust system and a very hot exhaust pipe (the author once saw his exhaust pipe actually glowing red due to temporary neglect in this matter!). The necessary adjustment of the exhaust valve lifter can readily be made by means of the adjustable cable stop provided for that purpose. See that the lock-nut is afterwards securely retightened.

Compression Release Valve. A compression release valve is not fitted on the 1934–8 two-strokes, but on some earlier models the cause of a loss of compression which cannot be traced in any other way will be found in the pitting of the compression release valve. This valve is similar to an ordinary four-stroke poppet valve in appearance, but is smaller, and has a much lighter spring. It seldom requires grinding in, but if it is desired to "touch it up" without removing the body, etc., from the cylinder, it can be rotated by removing the sparking plug and inserting a long screwdriver through the orifice. The slot in the head of the valve can be engaged and the valve gently turned on its seating.

Adjustment of Gear Control (Hand). Where hand control is provided it is necessary on all 1934–8 models except Model Z

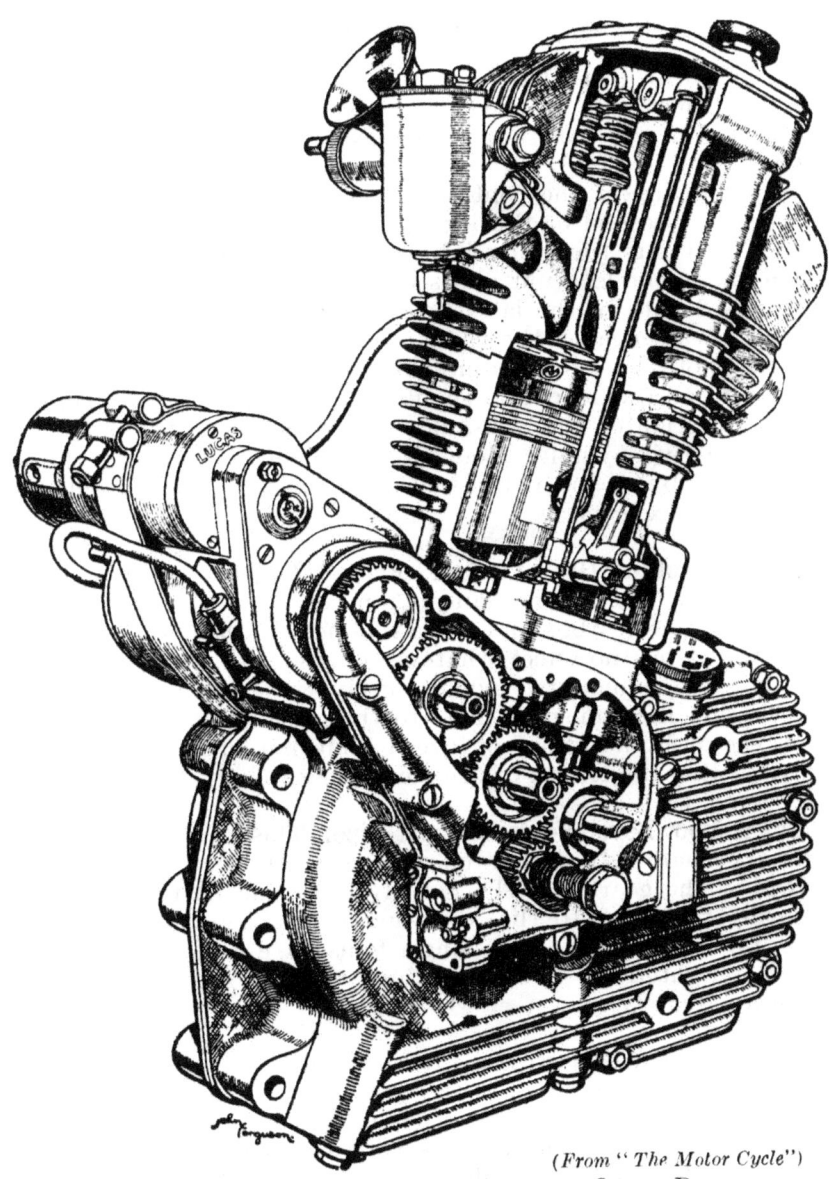

(*From "The Motor Cycle"*)

FIG. 54. SHOWING PUSH-ROD ADJUSTMENT AND OTHER DETAILS OF THE 1935 THREE-VALVE ENGINE (LO, LO2)

Except in regard to the cylinder head and overhead valve gear, this engine is identical to the 1934 four-valve engine (Model LF). Note besides the unusual valve clearance adjustment at the foot of each push-rod, the vertical arrangement of the three valves (two inlet and one exhaust, see opposite) which are enclosed in a rocker-box cast integral with the cylinder head and lubricated positively by means of an external feed from the pump; the down-draught Amal carburettor; the neat push-rod enclosure; the three-ring aluminium piston and the two-cam timing gear.

"Cycar" (which has hand control fitted direct to the gearbox) after adjusting the primary chain by moving the gearbox, to check and if necessary adjust the gear control. This is done as follows.

First disconnect the control rod at the quadrant lever, place the gears in second or third gear (second with three-speed gearboxes) and put the control lever in the corresponding notch. Then loosen the lock-nut and screw up or down the vertical rod until the length of the latter is adjusted such that with second or third gear engaged the hand control lever is perfectly free in the *centre* of the corresponding quadrant notch. This adjustment applies to all the gears and should be checked carefully. Do not forget to retighten the lock-nut securely on the forked end.

On the twin-cylinder Model K the length of the control rod is adjusted by means of the two nuts situated one on each side of the gearbox lever.

Adjustment of Gear Control (Foot). The foot control lever itself or the ratchet mechanism (on some models) is mounted directly on the gearbox and it is a *sine qua non* that primary chain adjustment has no effect whatever on the gear control. Where the foot lever is mounted independently of the gearbox (i.e. where the ratchet mechanism is fixed to the gearbox) it is possible to vary the position of the foot lever to suit individual requirements by adjusting the length of the connecting rod.

If the Foot Lever Fouls Exhaust Pipe. This can happen after primary chain adjustment on models where the lever is fixed direct to the gearbox. The remedy is to slacken the two nuts securing the lever to the operating mechanism and move the lever up or down until it no longer fouls the exhaust pipe. Afterwards retighten the two nuts, which must at all times be kept done up securely.

Clutch Control Adjustment. It is exceedingly important always to permit a small amount of free movement (about $\frac{1}{16}$ in.) of the clutch operating lever on the gearbox. Unless this free movement exists, some of the spring pressure is taken by the clutch wire instead of by the friction plates, with the result that the clutch slips, so damaging the friction cork inserts. On new machines these inserts bed down during the first 100 miles or so and the clutch control adjustment should therefore be frequently checked and if necessary adjusted.

Two types of clutch operating levers are used on 1934-7 models and these are shown in Figs. 55, 56. The adjustment is the same in each case, and is made thus: loosen the lock-nut *B*

ADJUSTMENTS AND OVERHAULING

and with a screwdriver rotate the adjusting screw A until the lever M has a free motion of approximately $\frac{1}{16}$ in. Finally retighten lock-nut B. For adjustment of 1938 clutch, see page 123.

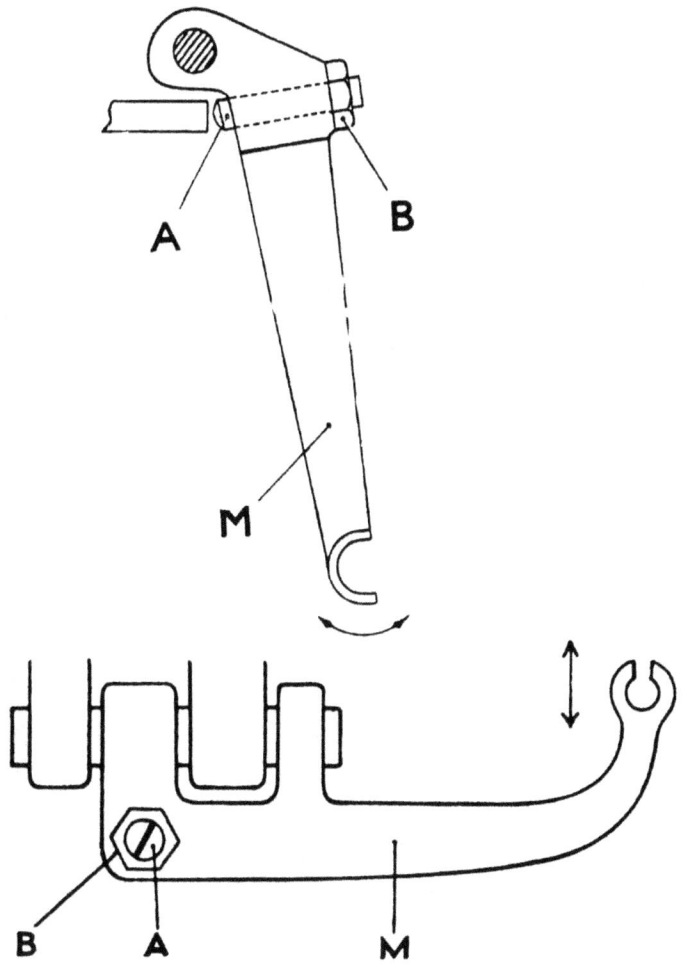

FIGS. 55, 56. SHOWING PROVISION FOR CLUTCH ADJUSTMENT
The operating lever shown above is used on some 1934-5 models and the type shown below on others. For 1938 type see Fig. 67.
A = Adjusting screw. B = Lock-nut. M = Operating lever.

If the Clutch Slips. First of all check the adjustment described on page 98. If this is in order, perhaps the cork inserts have become worn or burnt. In this case it is necessary to dismantle the clutch and have new inserts fitted. To remove the springs and plates it is only necessary to remove the primary chain cover or chain case (oil bath models) and unscrew the pins near the clutch centre, when the plates and springs can be lifted out. No adjustment is provided for the spring pressure and the screws should always be kept done up tight.

Do Not Worry About Oil on It. Cork inserts function equally well whether they run dry or greasy and therefore should oil or grease get on to the clutch, do not spend a sleepless night! As a matter of fact, since oily inserts naturally wear longer than dry ones, it is preferable on aluminium chain case models to keep the oil bath well filled.

Importance of Correct Chain Tension. It is important to keep both the primary and secondary chains correctly tensioned. Chains which are too slack are apt to rattle and jump the sprockets at a critical speed. On the other hand, chains which are too tight cause damage to the chain rollers and wear the chain sprockets quickly, the teeth becoming "hooked."

To Adjust Primary Chain. Pivot-mounted gearboxes are installed on all 1934-8 models and to adjust the primary chain it is only necessary to slacken the two securing nuts and then to pivot the gearbox about the lower of the two bolts holding the gearbox to the rear engine plates until the centre of the chain run has a free up and down movement of about $\frac{1}{4}$ in. when deflected by the fingers. On the oil-bath chain case models an inspection cover on the chain case gives immediate access to the chain. After retensioning the chain and tightening the gearbox nuts it may be necessary (see page 96) to readjust the gear control.

Secondary Chain Adjustment. The secondary chain should be kept adjusted so that there is approximately $\frac{1}{2}$ in. of free up and down movement. The chain gradually stretches and requires to be retensioned at certain intervals. To do this, slacken both rear wheel spindle nuts and then (except in the case of Model Z "Cycar," which has drawbolt adjusters) adjust the set pins in the fork ends until the correct chain tension is obtained. When adjusting the set pins (or draw bolts) see that the adjustment is carried out an equal amount on both sides of the fork ends, otherwise the wheel alignment (see page 90) will be disturbed. After adjusting the secondary chain it may be found necessary to make an adjustment to the rear brake (described in a later paragraph).

ADJUSTMENTS AND OVERHAULING

To Adjust Dynamo Chain (Model A). The chain should be kept adjusted so that it has the same free up and down movement as the primary chain, i.e. $\frac{1}{4}$ in. To adjust it, loosen the nut underneath the dynamo below the engine plates which holds the fixing strap and then turn the dynamo in its housing until the correct chain tension is arrived at.

" Magdyno " Chain Adjustment (Model K). On all machines except the Big Twin the "Magdyno" is gear-driven. On this

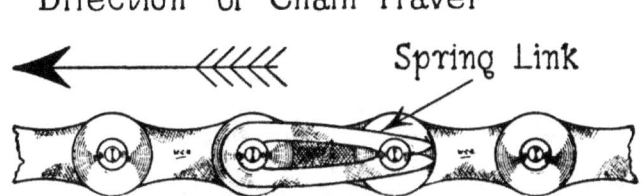

Fig. 57. Showing the Correct Way to Fit a Chain Spring Link

It is unsafe to fit the link with the open end facing the direction of chain motion.

machine to adjust the dynamo chain so that it has a free up and down movement of $\frac{1}{4}$ in., loosen the two bolts securing the "Magdyno" mounting to the engine plates and then tilt the mounting the necessary amount, afterwards retightening the two bolts.

When Refitting a Chain. Always see that the spring link is fitted so that the open end faces *away* from the direction of chain movement. This is important because should a chain part at high speed, particularly a secondary chain, there is no knowing what damage, personal and material, it may cause. The author once ran with a chain guard missing, and a chain parting at 30 m.p.h. caused a slap on the back sufficient to cause semi-consciousness!

Adjust Brakes to Give Maximum Efficiency. The front brake can be adjusted by means of a milled nut situated near the bottom fork links and the rear brake by means of a wing nut at the end of the brake operating rod. Always keep both brakes adjusted to give maximum efficiency by adjusting the nuts so that the brake shoes are in close contact with the drums and yet do not bind when the brakes are released. To test for free rotation of the wheels when adjusting the brakes it is advisable to jack up the wheels and spin them by hand.

If Grease gets on the Linings. Remove the brake shoes and wash their frictional linings thoroughly in petrol. Also clean the inside of the drums. The usual cause of grease getting on the linings is over-zealous lubrication of the wheel hubs. Greasy linings cause a very marked deterioration in braking efficiency. If the linings have become very smooth and polished, rough them up with a file, and if the linings are badly worn renew them. If you fit new linings yourself see that the rivet heads are absolutely flush with the linings.

Adjustment of Wheel Bearings. You cannot adjust the wheel bearings on any four-stroke models even if you wish to do so, because there is no adjustment provided! Single-row deep groove journal races designed for dealing with heavy radial and thrust leads are used instead of cone and cup bearings which are used only on Model Z "Cycar." See also page 124.

To adjust the cone and cup ball races (used for both wheels on Model Z "Cycar") proceed as follows—

It is advisable to remove the wheel first as this greatly facilitates an accurate adjustment being carried out. To adjust, loosen the lock-nut and then turn the screw-mounted cone until the wheel spindle can be readily spun by hand without any "grinding" sensation being felt. Do not tighten the cones excessively, or the balls and their races will wear quickly and the balls may even disintegrate.

Removing Front Wheel. First raise the wheel clear of the ground either by putting the machine on the central stand or both stands (never use a front stand alone), or else by slipping a suitable box underneath the crankcase. Then disconnect the front brake cable control, loosen the wheel spindle nuts, spring apart the front fork girders slightly, and with a little persuasion the wheel will slide out.

The Detachable Rear Mudguard. On all models rear wheel removal and tyre repairs are very greatly facilitated by the quickly detachable rear mudguard and carrier (where fitted). To remove the mudguard (see Fig. 3), slacken the four nuts securing the mudguard stays to the rear of the frame and lift the mudguard (and carrier) away. Nothing could be simpler.

Puncture Repairs in "Knock-out" Time. On 350 and 500 c.c. Models it is possible to repair a puncture in the rear tyre with amazing speed, thanks to the detachable mudguard (see above) and the knock-out rear wheel spindle which permits of a tube being removed or fitted without *removing* the wheel. To remove

ADJUSTMENTS AND OVERHAULING

a tube in "Brooklands" manner, proceed as follows: After detaching the mudguard remove the off-side spindle nut and push the spindle out of the other side. Then slightly spring apart the rear forks and slide out the knurled distance piece between the hub and the off-side fork end. If you now disconnect the brake rod from the slotted operating arm and also one end of the brake anchor arm you can now slip the tube out through the gap left on the off-side. Be careful not to put any strain on the rear wheel when the distance piece and spindle are removed.

To Remove Rear Wheel. After detaching the mudguard as described in a preceding paragraph, remove the pin retaining the brake anchor arm and the wing nut on the brake rod, disconnect the secondary chain at the spring link (see page 101), loosen the spindle nuts and slide the wheel out of the slotted fork ends, tipping it slightly in the case of Model Z "Cycar" when nearly out so as to disengage the peg from the brake anchor arm.

Adjusting Front Forks (Tubular Type). To take up side play in the front fork links, slacken the nuts on the front fork spindles and adjust the spindles by means of their squared ends. Avoid adjusting the forks so closely as to interfere with their free action. Each spindle has a right- and left-hand thread so that rotation of the spindle in one direction opens the fork links and rotation in the other direction closes them. The L.H. threads are situated on the off-side of the machine and the R.H. threads on the near-side, and the lock-nuts are slackened by rotation in the direction marked by the arrows on the fork links.

If a sidecar is fitted, the bottom fork links should be removed and the steering stem turned round so that the offset is to the front. On re-fitting the fork links the wheel will be located farther forward, giving delightfully light steering.

Adjusting Front Forks (Pressed Steel Type). The adjustment for the pressed steel forks fitted on the lightweight models is the same as for the tubular type, the adjustment of which is described above, except that the *front upper* spindle has *bushes* screwed on the fork spindle and it is necessary to adjust these bushes after slackening the lock-nuts until the correct adjustment is obtained (i.e. until side play has been eliminated).

To Take Up Steering Head Play. All Royal Enfield models have ball bearing steering heads of generous proportions and these rarely require any attention. Should it be found, however, on attempting to "shake" the handlebars that some play has developed it should be taken up *at once*, otherwise the balls will come in for a severe hammering, for which they are not designed. To take up play in the steering head, first of all obtain a suitable box and place it under the crankcase so that it takes the weight of the machine off the front wheel. Then in the case of the medium- and heavy-weight machines, slacken the pin which passes through the steering head clip and adjust the plated nut on top of the steering column until all up and down play has disappeared. Be careful not to tighten the nut so much that stiffness of steering is caused, as apart from the question of stability this is also deleterious to the balls in the bearings.

On the lightweight models a steering head clip is not fitted and it is only necessary in order to take up play in the steering head to unscrew the large plated nut on top of the steering column and then make the necessary adjustment by means of the lower nut. See that the upper nut is securely retightened after making the adjustment.

Shock Absorber Adjustment. Where finger adjustment is provided it is quite independent of the fork spindle adjustment described on page 103 and can, of course, be made in a few minutes. To obtain comfortable riding on average roads the best use should be made of the hand adjustment provided. It is best to adjust the shock absorbers so that they have little effect when weight is applied to the handlebars, yet exert a marked retarding effect on the fork rebound when the weight is removed.

Where hand adjustment of the shock absorbers is not provided it is necessary to adjust them by tightening the fork links as described on page 103.

The Steering Damper. Intelligent use should be made of this fitment while riding, and it is quite surprising to those not accustomed to the steering damper how effective it is in steadying the machine at fast speeds. Generally speaking, slacken off at low speeds and tighten at high speeds. The exception to the rule is the sidecar, where to obtain comfortable steering it is best always to have the damper tightened down to some extent.

Do not Ride Cramped Up. On long journeys a comfortable riding position makes all the difference between arriving at journey's end as fresh as a daisy or as tired as a transatlantic airman. Remember that although you cannot expect armchair comfort on a motor-cycle you can on Royal Enfields get a very considerable degree of comfort if you adjust the riding position to *your* physical make-up. It is possible to vary considerably the tilt of the handlebars and to adjust the footrests also. Further, the carburettor, brake and clutch controls can be adjusted on the handlebars to suit your requirements.

HOW TO DECARBONIZE

When Advisable. After the first 1000–1500 miles have been covered (on a new engine) and subsequently at intervals of about 2000–2500 (about 1500 on two-stroke engines) miles an engine usually exhibits signs indicating that it is advisable to decarbonize it. Gone is that youthful vivacity and power, and probably the machine begins to shy at quite ordinary gradients up which it normally romps in a care-free manner and shows its disapproval in no uncertain way by emitting a knocking or pinking noise. Accompanying these objectionable symptoms is a change from a crisp exhaust note to one which is distinctly "woolly" and tells you that the engine is not in a healthy condition. As soon as the engine behaves (or rather misbehaves) in the above manner, and especially if unprovoked knocking is apt to occur, you should dry-dock the machine, remove the cylinder(s) and/or the cylinder head(s) and decarbonize the engine and grind-in the valves if necessary. The last mentioned usually require attention every alternate decarbonizing. Decarbonizing is a long word, but the actual job is quite a short one and presents no difficulties if the following instructions are carefully observed.

What are Carbon Deposits Due To? Carbon deposits are due to a combination of three things: (*a*) burnt lubricating oil; (*b*) carbonizing of road dust; (*c*) incomplete fuel combustion. When decarbonizing it is always worth while inspecting the valve seatings and *if necessary*, grinding-in the valves. Removal of the valves incidentally facilitates thorough cleaning of the ports.

In connexion with decarbonizing there are three types of engines to consider: (*a*) the side-valve engines; (*b*) the overhead-valve engines; (*c*) the two-stroke engines. The general procedure is much the same in each case, although differences in design make the dismantling work somewhat different.

The Side-valve Engines. The side-valve engines are perhaps the easiest to decarbonize, and as all 1934–8 Royal Enfield engines have detachable cylinder heads above the level of the valves, it is only necessary to remove the heads in order to decarbonize. When it is desired to inspect the piston rings and piston, the cylinder barrel as well as the head must, of course, be removed. Although the valves can be removed with the cylinder in position, it is much better to remove the cylinder barrel for this purpose, and the removal of the head and barrel is advised every alternate decarbonizing.

The Overhead-valve Engines. All O.H.V. engines naturally have detachable heads and hence to decarbonize the engine and grind-in the valves it is only necessary to remove the head complete with valves, unless it is desired to examine the piston and rings, in which case the barrel also must come off. Cylinder head removal on all 1934-8 models except Models S, S2 entails preliminary removal of the petrol tank without disturbing the lighting panel wiring. On the above mentioned two models it is possible to remove the cylinder head and cylinder barrel *together* with the tank in position, but if it is desired to remove the head only the tank must first be removed.

The Two-stroke Engines. No detachable head is provided on the two-stroke engines and to decarbonize them it is necessary to remove the entire cylinder without disturbing the petrol tank. With regard to valves, it is a case of "we have no valves to A" (or Z!). The complete enclosure of the engine on Model Z "Cycar" does not hinder decarbonizing and the cylinder can be readily removed with the engine in position.

To Remove Petrol Tank (1934-5 O.H.V. Models BO, G, LF, and LO). To remove the petrol tank preliminary to decarbonizing it is quite unnecessary to disturb the wires to the lighting panel. All you have to do is to remove the panel by undoing the two fixing screws, disconnect* the wires attached to the bridge piece across the horseshoe-shaped resistance behind the switch and remove the bridge piece together with the resistance and the switch lever after undoing the central fixing screw. The panel, with the rest of the wires attached to it, will now slide through the slot in the tank when the latter is lifted off and laid on one side.

To Remove Petrol Tank (O.H.V. Models S, S2, 1935 LO2). This is required to enable the cylinder head to be removed leaving the cylinder barrel undisturbed. Get to work as follows: take away the handlebars and clips complete by unscrewing the two pins attaching the handlebar clips to the ball head yoke. Then unscrew the four tank securing pins and lift the tank back on to the saddle. The panel wiring (1935-7) need not be disconnected; the leads are long enough to enable the tank to be lifted back on to the saddle far enough to permit of the cylinder head being removed.

To Remove Petrol Tank (1934-5 Model Z " Cycar "). Petrol tank removal is not necessary for decarbonizing, but as we are on the subject of tanks here is the method of doing it. First take off the engine cylinder, as described on page 109. Now remove the filler cap, the collar below it and the nut just behind the front

* Before touching the wiring, as a precaution disconnect the battery (page 71).

ADJUSTMENTS AND OVERHAULING

saddle attachment. The tank can now be pushed downwards, but is a tight fit owing to the rubber packing.

To Remove Petrol Tank (1934-8 O.H.V. Model T). To prepare Model T for decarbonizing the tank should first be drained. Then remove the balance pipe which connects the two halves, unscrew the four tank support bolts and lift the tank back on to the saddle. The wires leading to the panel switch are made extra long to allow of this being done, and it is quite unnecessary to interfere with the wiring. 1938 models have no tank switch.

To Remove Cylinder Head (1934-8 S.V.). Unscrew the nuts holding the detachable head (or heads in the case of Model K) to the cylinder barrel and then lift directly off the studs. If stiff, give a sharp tap sideways with a mallet or suitable implement (do not use a hammer, or the brittle casting may be damaged).

To Remove Cylinder Head (1934-5 O.H.V. Models BO, G). Having removed the petrol tank as described in a previous paragraph, detach the exhaust pipe(s) and silencer(s), carburettor, sparking plug and exhaust valve lifter cable. Remove the four pins securing the overhead rocker housing and lift the housing off. Then unscrew the rocker housing support posts and lift the cylinder head gently off the barrel.

To Remove Cylinder Head (1934 O.H.V. Model LF). After removing the tank (page 106), plug, carburettor, exhaust pipes, silencer and exhaust valve lifter, disconnect the ends of the rocker return springs (see Fig. 53) and unscrew the four large nuts securing the rocker spindles, and also the five $\frac{3}{8}$ in. pins holding the rocker plates to the four-valve cylinder head. Next remove the plate on the near-side, prising it off gently if necessary with a screwdriver. For safety, it is advisable to replace the near-side rocker spindle nuts and washers. Then remove the front half of the off-side plates (the exhaust valve lifter lever comes away with it), followed by the rear half of the off-side plates, bringing the rockers with it. The push-rods may be lifted out of their tubes. Finally remove the cylinder head by unscrewing the four nuts situated below the second fin from the top and lift the head clear of the cylinder barrel.

To Remove Cylinder Head (1935 O.H.V. Models LO, LO2). After removing the tank (page 106), carburettor, exhaust pipe, silencer and detaching the exhaust valve lifter lever, unscrew the four nuts securing the cylinder head to the barrel, disconnect the oil pipe to the rocker-box, lift the head so that it just clears the retaining studs and turn it horizontally slightly to the right to enable the rocker bearing pin to be unscrewed and withdrawn. After withdrawing it, remove the rockers and push-rods and finally lift the head off the cylinder barrel.

To Remove Cylinder Head (1935-8 O.H.V. Models S, S2). In order to remove the cylinder head and barrel together and afterwards separate them, proceed as described underneath. If it is preferred to remove the detachable cylinder head only, proceed thus: remove the tank as described on page 106, disconnect the carburettor, exhaust valve lifter, exhaust pipe, silencer, and take off the overhead valve cover and remove the rockers from their bearings, after which the push-rods can be lifted out of their tubes. All that remains to do now is to unscrew the four nuts securing the head to the barrel and lift the former off.

To Remove Cylinder Head (1934-8 O.H.V. Model T). Firstly it is necessary to lift the petrol tank back on to the saddle as described on page 107. Then unscrew the large milled nut and remove the cover from the overhead valve gear. Also remove the central stud securing this cover and unscrew the eight pins attaching the rocker housing to the head and lift away the rockers and housing. The push-rods may now be pulled out of their tubes. Remove the exhaust pipe and silencer, the carburettor, sparking plug, and unscrew the four long sleeve nuts and lift the cylinder head off the barrel.

To Remove Cylinder Head and Barrel (1935-8 O.H.V. Models S, S2). On these, as has been mentioned above, removal of the petrol tank is not essential in order to remove the cylinder head, provided it is taken off together with the barrel, which is done as follows: first remove the cover from the overhead valve gear and preferably the centre stud securing it. Next remove the small plate from the side of the cylinder, turn the engine round until the exhaust valve opens, disconnect the exhaust valve lifter wire, unscrew the adjusting bush and pull the wire and case clear away from the cylinder. Then unscrew the four cylinder base nuts, put the piston at B.D.C. and lift off the cylinder barrel and head. The exhaust valve lifter lever will hold the exhaust push-rod in place, but the inlet push-rod will fall out.

As soon as the cylinder base clears the crankcase studs, turn the cylinder slightly until the inlet push-rod can be dropped behind the timing case and lifted away. The cylinder and head should then be carefully drawn off the piston together as described for the cylinder barrel on the S.V. engines. By undoing the

ADJUSTMENTS AND OVERHAULING

cylinder head nuts the barrel and head can then be parted. If it is desired to remove the cylinder head only, leaving the barrel in position, this necessitates removing the tank (page 106) and proceeding as described on page 108.

Removing Cylinder Barrel (1934-8 S.V.).

On the single-cylinder engines after removing the detachable head (page 107), remove the silencer and exhaust pipe, the carburettor, sparking plug, exhaust valve lifter cable and valve spring cover. On the twin-cylinder Model K, after removing both heads, detach the silencer and exhaust pipes and then proceed to remove the induction pipe complete with carburettor.

To remove the cylinder barrel or barrels, unscrew the four cylinder base nuts, place the piston at bottom dead centre and draw the cylinder carefully with both hands off the piston, taking care not to put any side strain on the connecting-rod or to allow the piston skirt to strike the connecting-rod or crankcase when the barrel comes away.

It is the safest course to wrap a rag round the connecting-rod as soon as the piston sees daylight so as to prevent damaging it and to prevent foreign matter entering the crankcase hole.

When withdrawing the cylinder barrel from the rear piston on the Big Twin it is necessary to lift it so that the top frame tube fits between two of the cylinder head studs (see page 123).

Removal of Cylinder Barrel (1934-8 O.H.V.).

Proceed exactly as described above for the S.V. engines.

To Remove Cylinder (1934-5 Model A Two-stroke).

Remove the exhaust pipe and silencer, carburettor (with the induction pipe) and sparking plug. Then unscrew the four cylinder base nuts, place the piston at the bottom of its stroke and lift the cylinder till the end of the gudgeon pin is exposed. Push out the gudgeon pin and lift the cylinder and piston away together.

To Remove Cylinder (1934-5 Model Z " Cycar ").

Despite the thorough enclosure of the power unit, it is very simple to remove the cylinder without disturbing the engine itself. Follow the following instructions: remove the stand and exhaust pipe and silencer complete (the stand may now be replaced). Remove the petrol pipe, carburettor and sparking plug. The two front cylinder nuts are now accessible with the small tube spanner provided. The rear of the cylinder is held down by two long bolts screwed upwards into the cylinder base, and are accessible from underneath the engine. Remove the cylinder holding down bolts and lift the cylinder clear of the front studs, incline forward and draw the cylinder off the piston as described for the S.V. engines.

Piston Removal. The gudgeon pin is of the fully floating type, i.e. free to rotate in the piston and connecting rod bush. The pin is held in position on most engines by means of two spring circlips which fit into grooves machined at each outer end of the gudgeon-pin hole through the piston. One of these circlips can easily be removed with the tang end of a file or a pair of round-nosed pliers. It is advisable not to again use the circlip after removal, but to fit a new one. On no account interchange the pistons on a twin-cylinder model, and mark them on the inside so that they are replaced correctly.

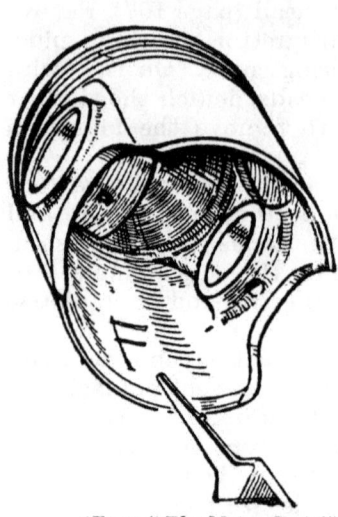

(*From "The Motor Cycle"*)
FIG. 58. MARK INSIDE OF PISTON TO ENSURE CORRECT REPLACEMENT

Each piston laps out the cylinder in which it fits in a certain way, depending upon the connecting rod thrust, lubrication, and other factors, and it is *never* advisable to alter its original position on the connecting rod. On the twin-cylinder S.V. engine mark the front piston "F," the rear piston "R," and so on. If the markings are scratched on the inside of the surface which faces the front there will be no doubt as to which is the correct way round to fit the piston on the connecting rod. On all the singles except the two-stroke (see p. 116) scratch the mark "F" as shown in Fig. 58 to indicate which is the front of the piston.

Piston Rings are Easily Broken. Great care must be taken when removing the piston rings as they are made of cast iron and are exceedingly brittle. It is unsafe to spring them out wider than the diameter of the piston crown, and the best method of removing the rings is shown in Fig. 59. Three strips of sheet tin about 1½ in. long and ⅜ in. wide are inserted under the rings opposite the slots, enabling the rings to be gently eased off one by one. Broken pieces of an old hack-saw blade will answer the same purpose. Be careful on the two-stroke engine not to damage the pegs.

The Piston Rings. The rings should be polished round the whole of their surfaces, and if either ring is discoloured or has a black

ADJUSTMENTS AND OVERHAULING

patch on it it means that gas has been leaking past, and it should therefore be replaced by a new one. With the rings removed the piston should be washed, so that the degree of carbon deposit in the slots may be readily seen. If any is found here it should be scraped away, but extreme care is necessary in order that the surface of the slot is not damaged by the scraping tool. If it is loss of compression will result, and if the slot is badly cut or

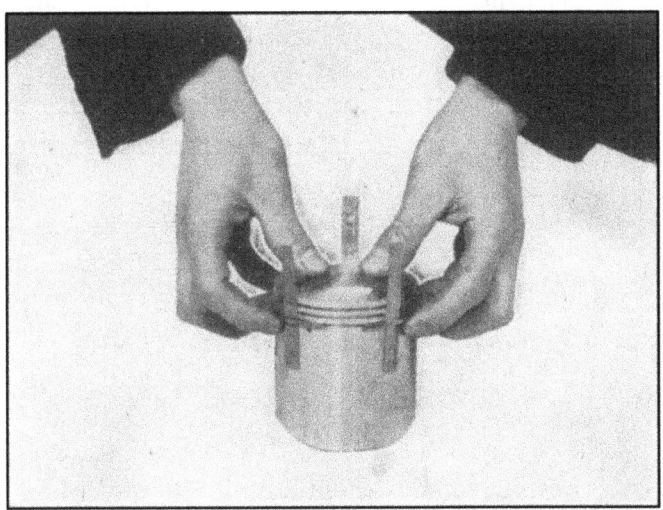

FIG. 59. THE SAFEST METHOD OF REMOVING PISTON RINGS

dented a new piston will probably have to be fitted for first-class results to be obtained. Any carbon deposit on the inside of the ring should also be scraped away. It is important to note that the rings should be quite free in their grooves, without much up-and-down movement. The piston and rings must again be washed in paraffin, after the carbon deposit has been removed.

Refitting the rings is quite a simple matter. Before this is done a few drops of oil should be placed in the slots and the top ring may then be pushed over the top of the piston until it is home, followed by the other rings. Alternatively the method shown in Fig. 59 may be used. See that the piston ring gaps are opposite each other. On a two-ring piston they should be spaced at 180 degrees and on a three-ring piston at 120 degrees. When replacing the piston rings it is important on the two-stroke piston to make sure that they fit freely in their grooves and that the pegs engage correctly in the gaps in the rings.

Removing the Carbon. Thoroughness in decarbonizing well repays the labour expended. The more completely the carbon is removed the better will the engine performance be, and the longer will it be before decarbonizing again becomes necessary. It is inadvisable, however, to decarbonize the piston ring grooves more than about once every alternate decarbonization, when the cylinder as well as the cylinder head should be removed. When undertaking an ordinary top overhaul, the carbon deposits on the piston crown and on the inside of the cylinder head need alone be scraped off. To do this, a suitable scraper such as the

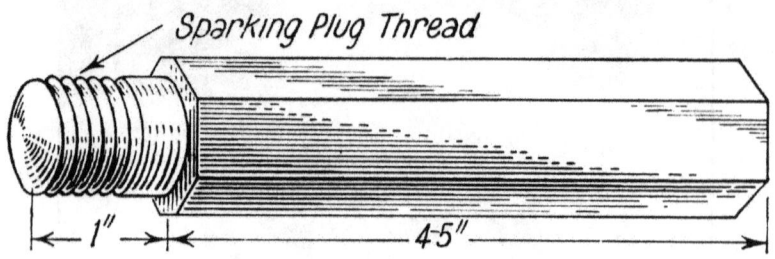

FIG. 60. A HEXAGON STEEL BAR TURNED AND THREADED AT ONE END TO HOLD A CYLINDER HEAD WHEN DECARBONIZING

On O.H.V. engines with integral cylinder head and rocker-box the head can be rested nicely on the top of the rocker-box and the above gadget is not required.

end of a screwdriver should be employed. Be careful, however, not to employ excessive force on the piston, or its comparatively soft aluminium surface will be deeply scratched. When decarbonizing the cylinder head, do not overlook the exhaust ports, which are usually heavily sooted or carbonized, and, as before mentioned, see that the face on the cylinder head is not scratched. A good method of holding the head on some engines when decarbonizing it is to fit a hexagon steel bar screwed at one end into the sparking-plug hole. Such a bar is shown in Fig. 60. The cylinder head may then be held in a vice by means of the bar. If a bar is unavailable, an old sparking plug makes a good substitute. After the deposits have been removed, clean the surfaces with a calico rag damped in paraffin.

In the case of the two-stroke models where the entire cylinder has to be removed, the top of the piston may afterwards be rubbed with *very fine* emery cloth until a perfectly smooth surface has been obtained. This method of finishing off may also be used for the detachable heads on all models, but the pistons should not be thus treated except when the cylinder itself is removed, enabling all abrasive particles to be afterwards eradicated. Emery particles which get down on to the rings may cause bad scoring of the cylinder walls. Polish the piston top with metal polish.

ADJUSTMENTS AND OVERHAULING

On the two-stroke models the deposits on the integral cylinder head may be reached through the cylinder mouth. Care should be taken not to allow the screwdriver shank to scratch the part of the cylinder included in the piston stroke. See also that all carbon is removed from the exhaust port, the piston ring grooves and the inside of the piston, and clean the silencer.

When occasion is had to remove the piston or pistons, do not attempt to remove carbon from the outside of the skirt. Only the crown, the inside, and the piston ring grooves should be scraped and cleaned. The latter may be cleaned of all deposits after the rings have been removed by running a small, sharp, flat-ended tool round their circumference. Only a tool of the right size should be used, or the shape of the grooves may be spoiled. A piece of broken piston ring can be used, but it is better to use a special tool.

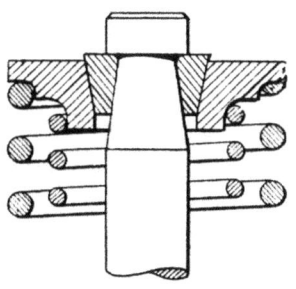

FIG. 61. SPLIT COLLET VALVE SPRING ANCHORAGE (Used on all Models except the Big Twin.)

To Remove the Valves (1934-8 S.V.). After removing the cylinder and cylinder head, removal of the valves can be readily undertaken for inspection of the valves and seats and subsequent grinding-in if necessary. Place the cylinder barrel upside down on the bench (or on a table or suitable box if you do not possess a bench), place a little soft packing below the valve heads so as to keep them firmly down on their seats, and then depress each valve spring by pressing down on the outer valve spring cap with a large screwdriver or suitable spanner until it is possible to remove the split collet (Fig. 61) from the tapered recess in the valve stem, or in the case of the twin-cylinder engine the flat cotter (Fig. 12) from the slot in the end of the stem. The valve spring, caps and valve may then be withdrawn.

On some engines it may be much more convenient to employ a proprietary valve spring compressor such as the "Terry" illustrated in Fig. 62A. The hooked end is rested on the centre of the valve head and the forked end of the lever slipped over the valve spring cap and the lever depressed until the valve spring is compressed sufficiently to enable the split collet or cotter, as the case may be, to be lifted out. If stuck, gently tap it out. With the tool illustrated it is possible to remove the valves with the cylinder barrel in position, but as it is always advisable to grind-in the valves with the cylinder barrel removed, there is no useful purpose served by doing so.

Do Not Interchange the Valves. Even if on some engines the valves are theoretically interchangeable, it is never in practice wise to change them over as each valve is ground into its individual seat and cannot be relied upon to form a gas-tight seal on a strange seat. Further, the highly stressed exhaust valve is usually made of extra special quality steel. If the valves are not

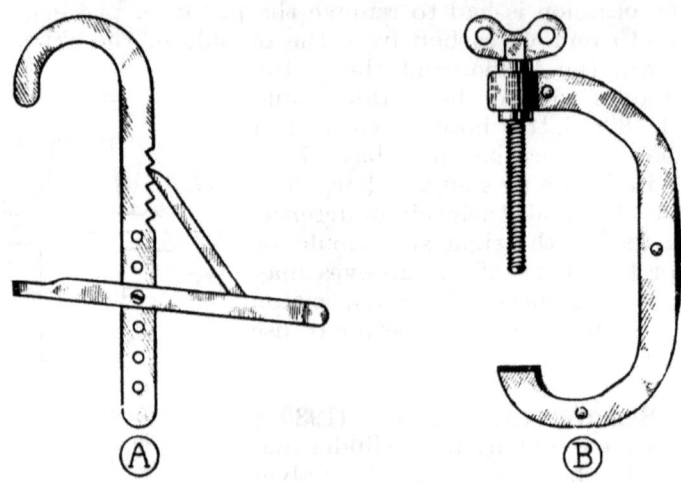

FIG. 62. TWO USEFUL VALVE SPRING COMPRESSORS
Both the above tools are obtainable from H. Terry & Sons, Ltd.
That shown at *A* is for S.V. engines and that at *B* for O.H.V. engines.

marked it is usually possible to identify the exhaust valve by the discoloration of the head due to heat. On the Big Twin it goes without saying that the valves should be marked to ensure correct replacement.

To Remove Valves (1934-8 O.H.V.). Owing to the different arrangement of the cylinder head the type of valve spring compressor shown in Fig. 62A is not suitable for compressing the valve springs on O.H.V. engines and it is necessary to employ a screw type compressor. A tool specially designed for O.H.V. engines (see Fig. 62B) is obtainable for a few shillings from Messrs. H. Terry & Sons, Ltd. The method of using this tool after first removing the hardened end caps on the valve stems is to place the forked end on the valve spring collar and the pointed end of the screw in the centre of the valve head and screw up until the valve spring is compressed sufficiently to enable the split collet to be removed. If stuck, gently tap it out. The valve spring collars and valve can then be removed. Deal with each valve similarly. As on the other engines, avoid interchanging the valves after removal and be most careful not to mix up the valves on the three- and four-valve engines.

Grinding in the Valves. Should the valve faces or seats show signs of serious pitting, the valves will have to be ground-in. Valves of the side-by-side and overhead type have, of course, to be rotated and lightly pressed down on their seatings with a screwdriver inserted in the slot in the valve head.

Only grind in valves when necessary, using a ready-made compound such as Richford's grinding paste; only a small quantity is necessary, and do not revolve the valves round and round, but rotate the valve about a third of a turn in one direction and then an equal amount in the opposite direction. About every six oscillations lift the valve, rotate it $\frac{1}{8}$ to $\frac{1}{4}$ of a revolution and proceed as before, stopping when no "cut" can be felt to redistribute the grinding paste and examine the valve face and seat. Continue grinding in until both the valve face and valve seat are quite bright. It will facilitate grinding-in the valves if a small compression spring is inserted under the valve head. This avoids the nuisance of having to repeatedly lift the valve by hand to change it to a new position. Very great care must be taken after grinding-in to remove all traces of valve-grinding compound. The valve stems may be cleaned with *very fine* or worn emery cloth. Do not use coarse grinding compound for grinding valves in unless the pitting is very extensive. A little fine paste smeared very lightly over the valve face is far better. Care should be taken to avoid burring the valve stems, otherwise unnecessary wear will take place in the valve guides.

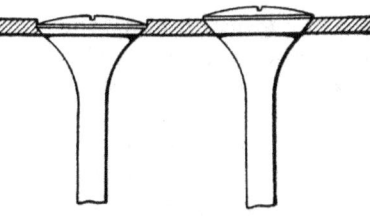

FIG. 63. SHOWING HOW VALVES BECOME POCKETED AFTER FREQUENT RE-GRINDING

Do not grind-in the valves to an unnecessary extent, as this eventually causes them to become "pocketed" (see Fig. 63), with the result that resistance is offered to the flow of the incoming and outgoing gases. See that all pitting is removed from each valve face and seat, but if the valves and their seats happen to be very badly pitted the proper course is to send the cylinder and valves to Redditch in order to have new faces cut.

Reassembling Valves. All is now ready for assembling. When replacing the valves see that the springs (duplex on O.H.V.), collars and cotters or split collets bed down properly. Replacing the valve springs is considerably helped on the single-cylinder engines by applying grease to the tapered portion of the valve stem as this enables the split collets to be held in place while compressing the springs with a "Terry" compressor or other suitable tool. On the three- and four-valve engines make sure that the individual valves are fitted into the seats into which they have been ground.

After Reassembling the Valves. It is an excellent plan to test the seats by pouring the petrol into the ports and watching for leakage past the valves. Not the slightest trace of moisture should creep past the valves until a very considerable time has elapsed. If some petrol does get past quickly it indicates that the valves have not been properly ground-in and the remedy is obvious—carry on.

Refitting Cylinder (S.V. and O.H.V.). Before starting to re-assemble, clean thoroughly all the parts with paraffin and clean rags. To refit the cylinder it is necessary to adopt roughly the reverse order of dismantling. If the crankcase on a 1934-6 Big Twin has been drained first pour some oil on to the flywheels and big-ends. Smear the cylinder wall and piston with clean engine oil before replacing the cylinder and see that the gudgeon pin circlip which has previously been removed is replaced by a new one and properly bedded down in the piston boss groove. When tightening down the nuts at the base of the cylinder, give each a successive turn in a diagonal order, otherwise there is a risk of distorting the cylinder base and preventing its bedding down properly on the crankcase. This method of tightening also applies to the cylinder head nuts. Before replacing the cylinder head it is advisable to coat the copper washer (where fitted) with shellac or other jointing compound so as to ensure a gas-tight joint. On the S.V. engines after refitting the carburettor, exhaust pipe, silencer and plug, check the valve clearances (page 93) and if necessary adjust them. Assembly is then complete. On the O.H.V engine it remains to replace the overhead valve gear, dealt with in a later paragraph.

Refitting Cylinder (Two-stroke). Satisfy yourself that all bits are clean and smear a little oil on the piston and cylinder before assembly. Then proceed to reverse the process of dismantling. On Model Z "Cycar" it will probably be found easier to push the piston partly into the cylinder before pushing the gudgeon pin through the piston bosses and little-end. See that the piston is fitted the right way round (the steep side of the deflector head to the rear). It is necessary to make an absolutely air-tight joint between the cylinder base and the crankcase (on the two-stroke

ADJUSTMENTS AND OVERHAULING

the mixture is compressed in the crankcase), and the contacting faces must therefore be quite clean and free from any traces of the old joint washer, which must be renewed. A paper washer is used and it should be oiled before insertion. When tightening the holding down bolts, tighten them diagonally and each a few turns at a time. Refit the carburettor, plug, exhaust pipe and silencer and you are "all set."

Replacing Overhead Valve Gear. This should present no difficulty if the reverse order of assembly is followed. See that the rocker housing support bolts are tightened evenly and securely and grease the push-rod ends before replacing. It is a good plan to insert the push-rods before refitting the cylinder head as this ensures that no difficulty is experienced due to spreading of the soft washers which seal the joints where the push-rod tubes and oil passages pass through it. If these soft washers appear at all damaged, fit new ones. On some 1934-8 O.H.V. engines the pushrods have deeper cups at the top than at the bottom and care should be taken to see that the push-rods are replaced with the deeper cups uppermost.

On the "R.E." four-valve engine the push-rods are readily engaged with the rockers if the near side rocker plate is fitted first. Before fitting the front half of the off-side plates on this engine, see that the push-rods are correctly replaced and do not forget the distance piece behind the back half of the off-side plate, and also the rocker return springs. Reassembly of the overhead rockers on the other O.H.V. engines is quite straightforward. On the 1935 three-valve engine fit the two rockers on the bearing pin and screw the pin firmly in place.

On all O.H.V. engines as soon as reassembly is complete it is necessary to check and/or adjust the valve clearances as described on pages 93-96, finally replacing the plug, valve cover, carburettor, exhaust pipe, silencer, etc. Once again the engine should spring into life on operating the kick-starter and the exhaust note should sound crisp and powerful after decarbonizing.

THAT ANNUAL OVERHAUL

About once a year most keen motor-cyclists strip down their "buses" and examine all the components, effecting such replacements and adjustments as an expert eye deems necessary. This annual overhaul, which of course, involves removing the engine and gearbox from the frame, is not a job to be undertaken lightheartedly by any except expert owner-drivers, and the following hints, necessarily brief, are only intended for those riders who have had some considerable experience. Others are advised to entrust the annual overhaul to expert hands.

Frame. Alignment, existence of flaws or cracks, play in fork links, looseness of steering head, wear caused by friction of all attached parts, condition of enamel.

Wheels. Condition of journal bearings or balls, cones, and cups; truth of wheels, alignment, loose spokes, condition of rims, wear of tyres, condition of valve "insides," wear of brake linings.

Chains. Excessive wear, cracked or broken rollers, joints, tension.

Engine. Oil leaks, compression leaks, main bearings, valves, valve guides and tappets, overhead valve rockers, valve springs, valve seats and faces, cotters, condition of cylinder bore, piston, piston rings, play in big-end and small-end bearings, timing wheels, shafts and bearings, cams, condition of plug and contact breaker.

Gears. Condition of teeth on sprockets and pinions, damaged ball races and loose parts generally.

The examination should also include all control rods and cables, tank filters, clutch and brake linings, etc. To sum up, everything should be dismantled and readjusted or renewed.

Removing Engine from the Frame (1934–5 S.V. and O.H.V.).

The following applies to all the single cylinder models.

Remove the exhaust pipe(s) and silencer(s), chain case, chain and all external fittings. To remove the lower half of the oil-bath chain case on some models, first take off the engine sprocket, when the case can be sprung past the end of the engine shaft. Now remove the bolts holding the engine into its plates and lower the front ends of the bottom frame members (on Models L, LF, LO, LO2). Remove the offside rear engine plate, leaving the large bolts still pushed through the near side plate and the frame lugs to hold the frame together. Machines having a central stand must be supported under the chain stays before the bottom frame members can be moved. The engine can now be lowered on to the floor, but is very heavy and some assistance may be required. Alternatively, the weight may be reduced by first removing the cylinder and piston. For 1936–8 engines, see page 125.

Dismantling the Crankcase (1934–8 S.V. and O.H.V.).

After removal of a single-cylinder engine from the frame, drain the oil tank and remove the cylinder and piston, if not already done. Next unscrew the timing cover screws and tap off the cover, then remove the magneto driving pinion. This is a taper fit on its shaft and is tapped for a small extractor, which will be found

ADJUSTMENTS AND OVERHAULING

in the tool kit. Now lift out the two cam wheels and the intermediate driving pinion(s) for the magneto or dynamo drive.

To remove the tappets and guides, tap them gently from underneath with a brass or aluminium drift (having first removed the tappet guide securing clamp on the side valve engines). Now loosen the dynamo (or "Magdyno") securing strap and lift the complete instrument away. Remove the timing pinion nut which

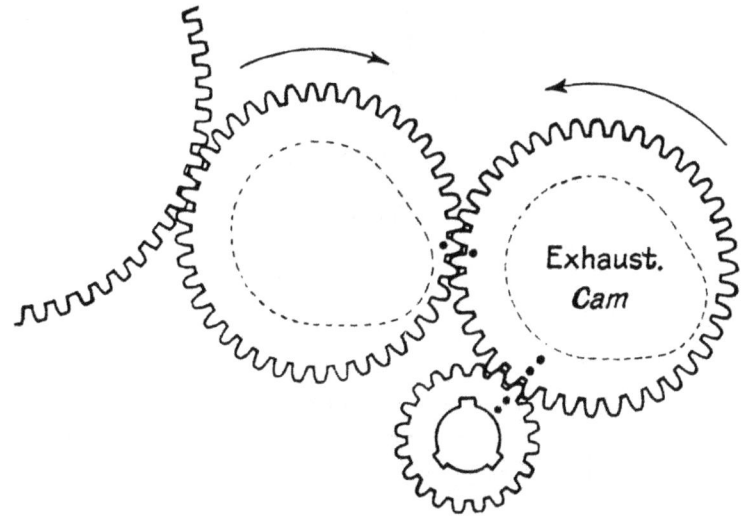

Fig. 64. Showing the Dot System Used for Marking the Valve Timing (1934-8 Singles)
(Note the three key-ways on the engine pinion enabling the timing to be varied by one-third of a tooth.)

has a left-hand thread. The pinion can now be drawn off the taper shaft (note the position of the key-way relative to the marking, see Fig. 64), preferably using a sprocket drawer. If one is not available, wedge a screwdriver behind the pinion and tap the end of the shaft, but take great care not to damage the shaft. It is now only necessary to remove the bolts holding the two halves of the crankcase together, when these can be separated. Do not lose the rollers from the main bearings as these fall out. Do not attempt to separate the flywheels.

Permissible Play in Engine Bearings. With the big-end and mainshaft roller bearings a small amount of end play is permissible, as is a little "shake" in the connecting-rod. If, however, quite appreciable up and down play can be felt it is advisable to send the crankcase, flywheels and connecting-rod to Redditch for attention as special appliances are wanted to ensure the correct assembly of new parts.

The gudgeon pin should be a free working fit in the small-end and a push fit in the piston bosses.

Valve Timing. No difficulty should be experienced when re-assembling the crankcase components, but care should be taken to see that all parts are quite clean and that the cams and bearings are oiled. The valve timing should be checked if the small engine pinion has been *removed* because it has three key-ways cut on it to enable the timing to be varied by one-third of a tooth (by using one or other of the key-ways), so enabling the exact timing to be obtained. Checking, however, can be dispensed with if note is taken of the key-way used prior to dismantling and if the dot system of marking the engine pinion, inlet and exhaust cam wheels (see Fig. 64) is used to obtain the correct relative positions of the three wheels. The valve timings for the 1934-6 Models are tabulated on this page and if in any doubt it is wise to check up the timing. Note that these timings are for checking with a valve clearance of ·005 in., and not the running clearances given on page 93. See also pages 123 and 128.

1934-6 VALVE TIMINGS (·005 in. CLEARANCE)

Model	Inlet Opens	Inlet Closes	Exhaust Opens	Exhaust Closes
S.V. (B, C, L) 1934-5	15° before T.D.C.	60° after B.D.C.	65° before B.D.C.	30° after T.D.C.
S.V. (K)	20° before T.D.C.	60° after B.D.C.	65° before B.D.C.	38° after T.D.C.
O.H.V. (BO, G) 1934-5	35° before T.D.C.	65° after B.D.C.	80° before B.D.C.	40° after T.D.C.
O.H.V. (S,S2, T)	30° before T.D.C.	60° after B.D.C.	75° before B.D.C.	35° after T.D.C.
O.H.V. (LF,)	35° before T.D.C.	65° after B.D.C.	65° before B.D.C.	35° after T.D.C.
O.H.V. (LO, LO2)	35° before T.D.C.	65° after B.D.C.	80° before B.D.C	40° after T.D.C.
S.V.(B,C,L,H) 1936	30° before T.D.C.	60° after B.D.C.	75° before B.D.C.	35° after T.D.C.
O.H.V. (G, J, JF)	30° before T.D.C.	60° after B.D.C.	75° before B.D.C.	35° after T.D.C.

Making Crankcase Joints. Use shellac, seccotine or any good proprietary jointing compound for the joint between the crankcase halves, and see that the special washer is used for the timing cover joint.

When Refitting Tappets. When refitting tappets and guides observe that the longer pair are for the exhaust valve.

Oil Pump Assembly. See notes on page 62.

APPENDIX

The foregoing instructions apply to 1934–8 models except where otherwise stated, but as there are certain omissions in regard to 1936–8 and 1939–40 models the following hints are given to bring the book completely up to date.

Valve Clearances (1936–8 S.V. Engines). On the 1936 9·76 h.p. Model K the same valve clearances should be given as for 1935 (·004 in., inlet; ·006 in., exhaust), but on the 1937–8 1140 c.c. Models K, KX the correct clearances are ·002 in. and ·004 in. for inlet and exhaust valves respectively. The adjustment in each case should be made with the engine *cold* in the manner described on page 94.

In the case of the 1936–8 single-cylinder S.V. engines (B, C, H, L) ·004 in. should be given for the inlet and ·008 in. for the exhaust valve with the engine *cold* (·002 in. and ·004 in. on 1936 Models B, C). Adjust the clearances as described on page 94. It should be noted that on the 1937–8 Big Twins and Model C the exhaust valve lifter prevents a spanner being applied to the tappet head and consequently the second spanner should be applied to the tappet body (bottom hexagon) when tightening or loosening the lock-nut. Adjust by turning the tappet body to left or right to lengthen or shorten the tappet respectively. In the case of a new machine, valve clearance adjustment is often called for after the first 100 miles, due to bedding down of the tappets.

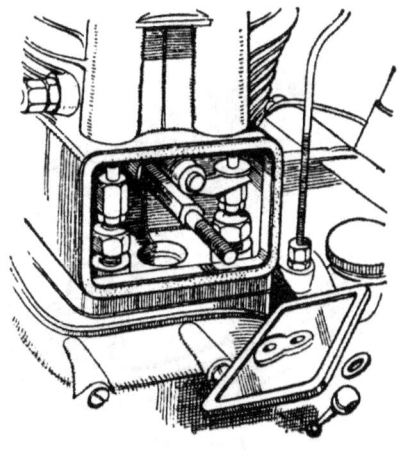

(*From "The Motor Cycle*)

Fig. 65. Tappet Adjustment on the 1936–8 O.H.V. Engines
(Applicable to all except Models JF, T)

Valve Clearances (1936–8 O.H.V. Engines). Tappet adjustment is provided on all 1936–8 O.H.V. engines except Models JF and T which have an overhead rocker adjustment, and access to the tappets (Fig. 65) is immediately obtained on removing the tappet cover from the side of the cylinder. The correct clearances with a *cold* engine are: inlet, *nil* (tappet just free to rotate); exhaust, ·004 in. On the 250 c.c. and 350 c.c. "Bullets," however, clearances of *nil* and ·002 in. are recommended. On all models except Models JF, T and the "250," "350" "Bullets" the valve clearances should be adjusted as described on page 94 for the S.V. engines (see also above paragraph regarding exhaust lifter on Models C, S, S2). The clearance at the exhaust tappet may be checked with a feeler gauge on removing the rocker-box cover.

To adjust the valve clearances on 1936–8 Models JF, T, proceed as described on page 95 for the 1934–5 Models LF, T respectively. On Model JF it should be possible to insert a single thickness of tissue paper between the adjuster screw and the valve stem. With the 250 c.c. and 350 c.c. "Bullets" loosen the tappet locknut and turn the adjuster screw with the squared end until the correct clearance is obtained.

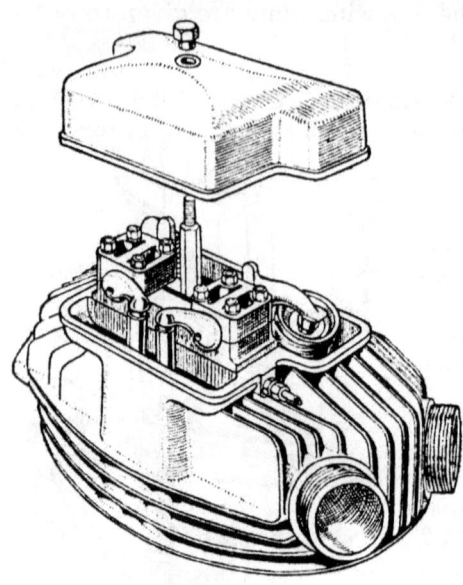

(*From "The Motor Cycle"*)

FIG. 66. SHOWING TWIN-PORT CYLINDER HEAD AND OVERHEAD VALVE GEAR ON THE 1937-8, 500 C.C. "BULLET."

To Remove Cylinder Head (1936 Model JF). Proceed as described on page 107 for the 1934 Model LF.

To Remove Cylinder Head (1936–8 Models G, G2, J, J2 and Competition Model). First of all the petrol tank must be removed. The wires to the lighting panel on 1936–7 models need not be disturbed as they are sufficiently long to allow of the tank being lifted back on to the saddle. Disconnect the headlamp wires if necessary from the lamp. Having removed the tank, proceed to remove the valve gear cover, the carburettor and the exhaust system. Next remove the rocker bearing caps and rockers and lift the push-rods from their tubes. It is then possible to lift off the cylinder head gently after unscrewing the four fixing nuts. In the case of the 1937–8 Model G there are five cylinder base nuts (four on 1936 models), and cylinder removal is straightforward after disconnecting the exhaust valve lifter (G, J) and putting the piston on B.D.C.

APPENDIX

To Remove Cylinder Head (1937-8 250 and 350 c.c. " Bullets ").

The petrol tank must first be drained and removed. Since there is not too much room to spare, removal of the rocker housing and cylinder head is greatly facilitated if the five cylinder holding-down nuts (one is placed between the tappet guides) are first removed, the exhaust pipe and carburettor taken off and the cylinder lifted clear of its studs and turned round so that the *push-rods face the front*. The rocker housing may now be removed after taking out the four securing pins. Next detach the push-rods from the tubes cast in the cylinder, remove the four cylinder head nuts and lift the head off the cylinder barrel. Should difficulty be experienced in getting the push-rods past the head joint, lift the rods away with the head.

Removing Cylinder Barrel (1937-8 Models K, KX).

Instructions for dismantling prior to decarbonizing are given on page 109. Follow these except the last paragraph dealing with removal of the rear cylinder. On the 1937-8 Big Twins it is best to unscrew the three back cylinder head studs before attempting to remove the rear cylinder. Mark each piston (see page 110).

Valve Timings (1937-8).

As hitherto, the timing gears are marked on all engines. On single-cylinder models two dots on the engine pinion should register with two on the exhaust camwheel, and the single dot on the exhaust camwheel should register with the single dot on the inlet camwheel (Fig. 64). Three key ways are provided on the engine pinion (see page 120).

1937-8 VALVE TIMINGS (·005 IN. CLEARANCE)

Model	Inlet Opens	Inlet Closes	Exhaust Opens	Exhaust Closes
S.V. (K, KX)	20° before T.D.C.	60° after B.D.C.	65° before B.D.C.	38° after T.B.C.
S.V. (B, C, L, H)	30° before T.D.C.	60° after B.D.C.	75° before B.D.C.	35° after T.D.C.
O.H.V. (T, S, S2)	30° before T.D.C.	60° after B.D.C.	75° before B.D.C.	35° after T.D.C.
O.H.V. (G, G2, J, J2)	30° before T.D.C.	60° after B.D.C.	75° before B.D.C.	35° after T.D.C.
500 Comp.	50° before T.D.C.	60° after B.D.C.	75° before B.D.C.	35° after T.D.C.

The 1938 Clutch Adjustment.

Referring to Fig. 67, the new type of clutch is adjusted in the following manner. First disconnect the lever M from the cable, and hinge it back to expose the adjuster screw A and sleeve B. Turn the screw A to the left to give more clutch backlash and turn it to the right to take up play. Correctly adjusted, the lever should have about $\tfrac{1}{16}$ in. free movement. No lock-nut is provided, since the screw and sleeve are automatically locked by the lever M when this is in position and the control cable is connected up.

Removing 1938 Model K Rear Wheel. Put the machine on the rear stand and after removing the detachable rear mudguard (Fig. 3) take out the pin securing the brake anchor arm, remove the wing nut on the rod, disconnect the rear chain, loosen the wheel spindle nuts and allow the wheel to slide out of the fork end.

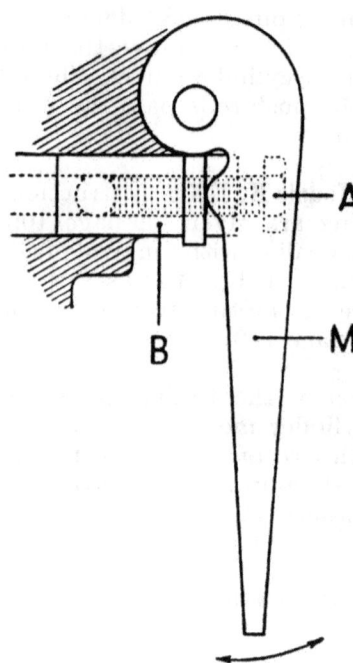

Fig. 67. The 1938 Clutch Control
(Fitted to heavyweight gearboxes only)

Removing 1937-8 Model K Front Wheel. Put the machine on both stands, disconnect the brake control, loosen the spindle nuts, spring out the forks slightly and let the wheel come away.

To Remove 1938 Model KX Detachable Wheels. Either wheel may be removed as follows. Place the model on the stand(s), unscrew the three pins G and the nut H (see Fig. 68). Then knock out the spindle J and slide the distance piece K out of the fork end. Next pull the wheel over to the side of the machine until the three pegs L are disengaged from the recesses in the cush drive centre F. The wheel can now be removed, leaving the brake in place (also cush drive and sprocket of the rear wheel).

When refitting the wheel, push the spindle J almost into place in order to steady the wheel prior to engaging the pegs C with their recesses. Fit distance piece K and tighten nut H *before* tightening the three pins G. Be sure to tighten them evenly so as to pull the wheel squarely on to the conical seating of the cush drive centre F.

Adjusting Wheel Bearings (1937-8 Models K, KX). Model **K** has taper roller bearings which are correctly adjusted at the Works, and should never require attention. If, however, the adjustment should accidentally be disturbed they can be readjusted by loosening the locknut inside the near-side fork end and turning the adjusting nut. This type of bearing must have little play, and it

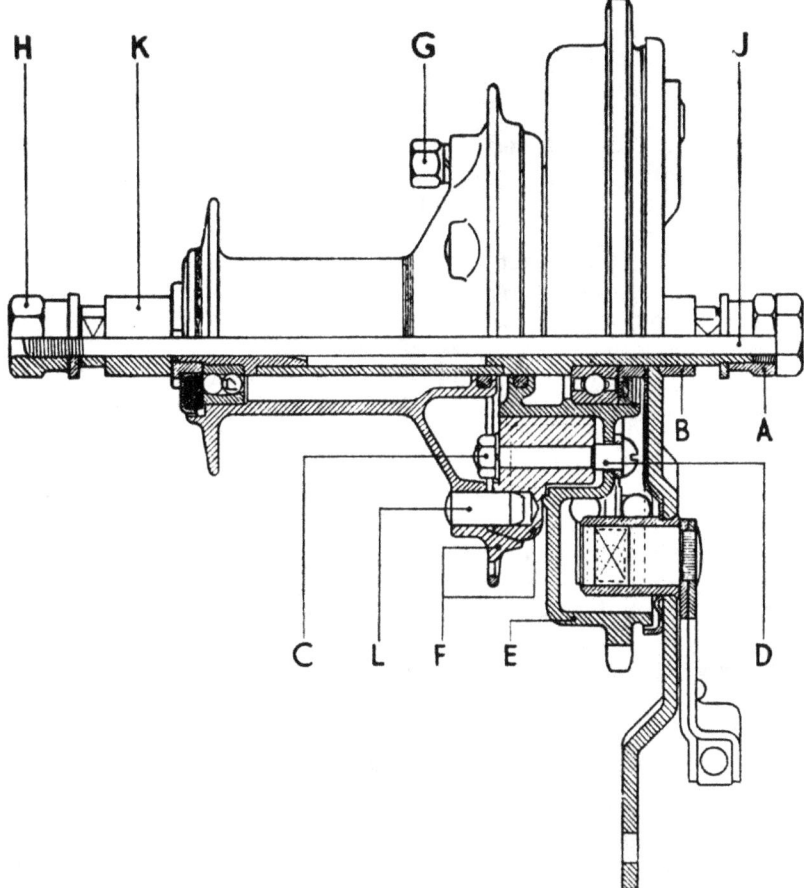

Fig. 68. Details of the 1938 Model KX Detachable Wheel Hub

should just be possible to feel a trace of side movement at the rim. The best procedure is to remove the wheel and adjust the bearings so that the spindle can be turned freely with the fingers.

Model KX is fitted with non-adjustable journal ball races which never require attention.

Removing Engine from the Frame (1936-8 S.V. and O.H.V.).

Remove the exhaust pipes and silencers, chain case, chain and all external fittings. To remove the front half of the chain unscrew the nut holding the near-side footrest, remove the footrest and brake pedal and pull the front of the case away from the rear half. To remove the rear half of the case first take off the engine sprocket, clutch and primary chain. Then unscrew the small pin securing the case to the engine and the two nuts securing it to the gearbox attachment bolts and lift the case away. Now remove the bolts holding the engine into its plates. Remove the off-side engine plate and lift the engine out of the frame.

Dismantling Four-speed Gearbox. The gears on the four-speed gearbox cannot be removed until the mainshaft has been withdrawn, and to do this the clutch must be taken off.

Remove two bolts holding on bearing cap and remove cap complete with clutch actuating lever. The mainshaft nut is *left hand*, and must therefore be unscrewed in a clockwise direction. The cover bolts may now be removed and the cover lifted off. Do not prise cover by means of a screwdriver, as this damages the face of the cover and destroys the joint, causing oil leaks. A gentle tap on the clutch end of the spindle with a mallet will loosen it. The kick starter mechanism comes away with the cover. The mainshaft can now be withdrawn, followed by the layshaft, layshaft gears, mainshaft sliding gears and fork in one block. The withdrawal of the mainshaft sleeve and sleeve gear completes the dismantling as far as is necessary for practically everything.

In all cases, when assembling, make sure that the ball of the operator, which juts out of the box, fits into the operator lever which is in the cover. The chain sprocket is mounted on the high gear sleeve by means of splines and locked down by a key washer and lock ring. These are unscrewed with an anti-clockwise movement.

MAINTENANCE (1939–40 Models)

Suitable Engine Oils. The recommendations given on page 52 hold good, but it should be noted that Price's Motorine B De Luxe is also suitable, and that Patent Castrol XL (not XXL) should be used on the two-stroke Model A.

The 250 c.c. Lubrication System. Models D, S, SF which have circular crankcases have a normal type of worm-driven double-acting plunger pump as used on the other singles, giving a force feed to the big-end, the timing gear and the rocker-box (via an external pipe). The oil, however, is not carried in a sump integral with the crankcase, but is contained in a separate oil tank mounted neatly between the rear engine plates. Oil from the timing case and oil trapped in a small well at the rear of the crankcase is returned by the pump to the tank which has a drain plug and also a detachable gauze filter. The level of oil should be maintained

APPENDIX

as high as possible, but it should not rise above 1 in. below the return pipe orifice where the circulation may be verified. On no account allow the level to drop below the bottom of the gauze filter in the filling orifice. Drain the tank about every 1500-2000 miles and replenish with fresh oil. Also clean the filter by brushing with paraffin. No adjustment is provided and the valve guides are automatically lubricated. On other machines the lubrication system is unchanged.

FIG. 70. ROYAL ENFIELD TWIN CAMWHEEL TIMING GEAR
The exhaust camwheel and flat base tappet are shown removed. On the 250 c.c. models with circular crankcases a single camwheel with twin cams is used.

Miller Dynamo Lubrication. The new Miller dynamo used on coil-ignition models (all except A, T) has a small oil lubricator on the driving end and a grease nipple in the centre of the contact-breaker cam for greasing the reduction gears driving the cam. Lubricate sparingly every 500 miles.

Dealing with Air Filters. Box-type air filters are fitted on Models C, J, G, J2. Renewal of the filter element is not needed, but it should be washed with petrol and dipped in clean oil every 2000-3000 miles.

Sparking Plugs for 350 c.c. "Bullet." For running-in a Lodge H14 or K.L.G. L583 is suitable, but for continuous hard work it is best to fit a Lodge H53 or a K.L.G. 831.

Correct Tyre Pressures. The correct solo pressures for the (Dunlop) tyres on Model D are 16 lb. per sq. in. and 24 lb. per sq. in. for front and rear tyres respectively. In the case of the 350 c.c. "Bullet" (Model G), inflate to 18 lb. per sq. in. and 22 lb. per sq. in. respectively.

Miller Switch Positions. The switch positions on the coil-ignition set are as follows: "PK" (pilot and tail); "OFF" (ignition and lights off); "IG & CH" (ignition on, lights off; "H" (main bulb, tail and ignition on); "L" (pilot, tail and ignition on).

Miller Bulb Replacements. The correct bulb replacements for machines with Miller coil ignition are: headlamp, 6 volt, 18 watt; pilot and tail lights, 6 volt, 3 watt.

The Miller Contact-breaker. Keep the gap adjusted to 0·018 in. Occasionally grease the cam slightly and clean the contacts with a petrol-soaked rag. Polish the lever spindle if sluggish. The dynamo bearings are packed with grease on assembly. Do not meddle with the voltage regulator.

1939 Valve Clearances. The correct valve clearances for all single-cylinder S.V. engines are 0·004 in. and 0·008 in. for the inlet and exhaust valves respectively *with the engine cold*. Adjust the tappets as described on page 94. On all O.H.V. engines except the 350 c.c. "Bullet" give a clearance of *nil* for the inlet and 0·004 in. for the exhaust valve, *with the engine cold*. In the case of 350 c.c. "Bullets," a clearance of *nil* is advised for *both* valves. Adjustment is provided at the base of the push-rods as for 1938 (incorrectly stated on page 122), except in the case of the four-valve cylinder head available as an extra on the 500 c.c. "Bullet" and the Competition model. On four-valve models overhead rocker adjuster screws and lock-nuts (Fig. 53) are fitted.

Decarbonizing Hints. Follow the instructions given for corresponding 1938 models. Copper cylinder head gaskets are fitted on all models except the 350 c.c. "Bullet." Petrol tank removal is advised prior to dismantling the engine of this machine and Model SF. Dismantling the 350 c.c. "Bullet" is straightforward, but note that the cylinder head is held to the barrel by six studs and nuts, some of which are not accessible until after

APPENDIX

removal of the caps over the inlet and exhaust rockers. There is not quite sufficient clearance to lift the head off the barrel and therefore the two should be removed *together*.

Ignition and Valve Timings. Ignition timings are the same as for the corresponding 1938 models (see page 45). On the 350 c.c. "Bullet" the contacts should begin to open $\frac{1}{2}$ in. before T.D.C. on full advance. Valve timings are unchanged except on the machines with circular crankcases (Models D, S, SF) and single-camwheel timing gear. In this case the correct timing is as follows: inlet opens 22° before T.D.C.; inlet closes 60° after B.D.C.; exhaust opens 60° before B.D.C.; exhaust closes 22° after T.D.C. On the new 350 c.c. "Bullet" the timing is: inlet opens 30° before T.D.C.; inlet closes 60° after B.D.C.; exhaust opens 75° before B.D.C.; exhaust closes 35° after T.D.C. Three key-ways are provided on the engine pinion as hitherto.

Front Fork Spindle Adjustment. Adjustment of the tubular fork spindles is the same as for 1938 (page 103), except that in the case of the new tubular forks on Models T, D, S, SF the adjustment for the *top* links is the same as for the top links on the 1938 pressed-steel type.

Other Maintenance Matters. Beyond the above-mentioned points the instructions given in the earlier parts of the book are generally applicable to 1939–40 models.

INDEX

ALIGNMENT, wheel, 90
Amal carburettor, principle of, 32, 38
——— ———, tuning, 34, 39
Ammeter, 72
Annual overhaul, 117

BATTERY maintenance, 72
Bearings, play in, 119
Brake adjustment, 101
Bulb replacements, 76

CARBON deposits, 105
———, removing, 111
Carburettor, 31
——— flooding, 37
Chain adjustment, 100
——— lubrication, 67
Charging battery, 76
Clutch adjustment, 98
Coil ignition, principle of, 43
Commutator, 72
Compression release valve, 96
Contact breaker, 46–48
Crankcase, dismantling, 118
Cush drive rear hub, 6
Cut-out, 71
Cylinder head, removing, 107
———, removing, 109

DECARBONIZING, 105
Draining crankcase, 56, 64
——— oil tank, 62
Driving licence, 9, 11, 26
Dry sump lubrication, 60
Dynamo, care of, 69, 81
——— contact breaker, 48
——— lubrication, 65

ENGINE oils, suitable, 52
Exhaust valve lifter, 96

FOCUSING lamps, 79, 85
Forks, adjusting, 103
Four-stroke engine, principle of, 22

GEAR changing, 15
——— control adjustment, 96
Gearbox lubrication, 65
———, principle of, 29
Grinding-in valves, 115

HUBS, lubrication of, 67

IGNITION, timing, 44
——— warning lamp, 49

LODGE plugs, recommended, 49
Lubrication, 51
——— chart, 66

"MAGDYNO," care of, 46, 64, 69
Magneto, principle of, 41
Mechanical pump lubrication, 52

OVERHEAD valve gear, lubricating, 64

PETROIL lubrication, 58
Petrol tank, removing, 106
Pilgrim pump, 52
Piston removal, 110
——— rings, 110

REPLENISHMENT, oil, 62

SHOCK absorber adjustment, 104
Sidecar alignment, 91
Sight feed, 54
Sparking plug, 49
Specific gravity, acid, 73
Steering head, play in, 103
Switch positions, headlamp, 75, 84

TAPPET adjustment, 94
"Third brush" control, 69
Timing, ignition, 44
Topping up battery, 72
Tuning Amal carburettor, 34, 39

Two-stroke engine, principle of, 28
—— —— lubrication, 58
Tyre pressures, 88

VALVE clearances, 93
—— timing, 120

Valves, removing, 113

WARNING lamp, ignition, 49
Wheel bearings, adjusting, 102
—— removal, 102
Wiring diagrams, 74, 77, 78, 80

AUTOBOOKS WORKSHOP MANUALS

ALFA ROMEO GIULIA 1300, 1600, 1750, 2000 1962-1978 WSM
BMW 1600 1966-1973 WSM
BMW 2000 & 2002 1966-1976 WSM
BMW 2500, 2800, 3.0 & 3.3 1968-1977 WSM
BMW 316, 320, 320i 1975-1977 WSM
BMW 518, 520, 520i 1973-1981 WSM
FIAT 1100, 1100D, 1100R & 1200 1957-1969 WSM
FIAT 124 1966-1974 WSM
FIAT 124 SPORT 1966-1975 WSM
FIAT 125 & 125 SPECIAL 1967-1973 WSM
FIAT 126, 126L, 126 DV, 126/650 & 126/650 DV 1972-1982 WSM
FIAT 127 SALOON, SPECIAL & SPORT, 900, 1050 1971-1981 WSM
FIAT 128 1969-1982 WSM
FIAT 1300, 1500 1961-1967 WSM
FIAT 131 MIRAFIORI 1975-1982 WSM
FIAT 132 1972-1982 WSM
FIAT 500 1957-1973 WSM
FIAT 600, 600D & MULTIPLA 1955-1969 WSM
FIAT 850 1964-1972 WSM
JAGUAR E-TYPE 1961-1972 WSM
JAGUAR MK 1, 2 1955-1969 WSM
JAGUAR S TYPE, 420 1963-1968 WSM
JAGUAR XK 120, 140, 150 MK 7, 8, 9 1948-1961 WSM
LAND ROVER 1, 2 1948-1961 WSM
MERCEDES-BENZ 190 1959-1968 WSM
MERCEDES-BENZ 220/8 1968-1972 WSM
MERCEDES-BENZ 220B 1959-1965 WSM
MERCEDES-BENZ 230 1963-1968 WSM
MERCEDES-BENZ 250 1968-1972 WSM
MERCEDES-BENZ 280 1968-1972 WSM
MG MIDGET TA-TF 1936-1955 WSM
MINI 1959-1980 WSM
MORRIS MINOR 1952-1971 WSM
PEUGEOT 404 1960-1975 WSM
PORSCHE 911 1964-1973 WSM
PORSCHE 911 1970-1977 WSM
RENAULT 16 1965-1979 WSM
RENAULT 8, 10, 1100 1962-1971 WSM
ROVER 3500, 3500S 1968-1976 WSM
SUNBEAM RAPIER, ALPINE 1955-1965 WSM
TRIUMPH SPITFIRE, GT6, VITESSE 1962-1968 WSM
TRIUMPH TR2, TR3, TR3A 1952-1962 WSM
TRIUMPH TR4, TR4A 1961-1967 WSM
VOLKSWAGEN BEETLE 1968-1977 WSM

VELOCEPRESS AUTOMOBILE BOOKS & MANUALS

ABARTH BUYERS GUIDE
AUSTIN-HEALEY 6-CYLINDER WSM
AUSTIN-HEALEY SPRITE & MG MIDGET 1958-1971 WSM
BMW 600 LIMOUSINE FACTORY WSM
BMW 600 LIMOUSINE OWNERS HAND BOOK & SERVICE MANUAL
BMW ISETTA FACTORY WSM
BOOK OF THE CARRERA PANAMERICANA - MEXICAN ROAD RACE
COMPLETE CATALOG OF JAPANESE MOTOR VEHICLES
CORVAIR 1960-1969 OWNERS WORKSHOP MANUAL
CORVETTE V8 1955-1962 OWNERS WORKSHOP MANUAL
DIALED IN - THE JAN OPPERMAN STORY
FERRARI 250/GT SERVICE AND MAINTENANCE
FERRARI 308 SERIES BUYER'S AND OWNER'S GUIDE
FERRARI BERLINETTA LUSSO
FERRARI BROCHURES AND SALES LITERATURE 1946-1967
FERRARI BROCHURES AND SALES LITERATURE 1968-1989
FERRARI GUIDE TO PERFORMANCE
FERRARI OPP, MAINTENANCE & SERVICE H/BOOKS 1948-1963
FERRARI OWNER'S HANDBOOK
FERRARI SERIAL NUMBERS PART I - ODD NUMBERS TO 21399
FERRARI SERIAL NUMBERS PART II - EVEN NUMBERS TO 1050
FERRARI SPYDER CALIFORNIA
FERRARI TUNING TIPS & MAINTENANCE TECHNIQUES
HENRY'S FABULOUS MODEL "A" FORD
HOW TO BUILD A FIBERGLASS CAR
HOW TO BUILD A RACING CAR
HOW TO RESTORE THE MODEL 'A' FORD
IF HEMINGWAY HAD WRITTEN A RACING NOVEL
JAGUAR E-TYPE 3.8 & 4.2 WSM
LE MANS 24 (THE BOOK THAT THE FILM WAS BASED ON)
MASERATI BROCHURES AND SALES LITERATURE
MASERATI OWNER'S HANDBOOK
METROPOLITAN FACTORY WSM
MGA & MGB OWNERS HANDBOOK & WSM
OBERT'S FIAT GUIDE
PERFORMANCE TUNING THE SUNBEAM TIGER
PORSCHE 356 1948-1965 WSM
PORSCHE 912 WSM
SOUPING THE VOLKSWAGEN
SOLEX CARBURETORS (EMPHASIS ON UK & EU AUTOMOBILES)
SU CARBURETORS (EMPHASIS ON UK AUTOMOBILES)
TRIUMPH TR2, TR3, TR4 1953-1965 WSM
TUNING FOR SPEED (P.E. IRVING)
VEDA ORR'S NEW REVISED HOT ROD PICTORIAL
VOLKSWAGEN TRANSPORTER, TRUCKS, STATION WAGONS WSM
VOLVO 1944-1968 ALL MODELS WSM
WEBER CARBURETORS (EMPHASIS ON ALFA & FIAT)

BROOKLANDS BOOKS & ROAD TEST PORTFOLIOS (RTP)

AC CARS 1904-2009
ALFA ROMEO 1920-1933 ROAD TEST PORTFOLIO
ALFA ROMEO 1934-1940 ROAD TEST PORTFOLIO
BRABHAM RALT HONDA THE RON TAURANAC STORY
BUGATTI TYPE 10 TO TYPE 40 ROAD TEST PORTFOLIO
BUGATTI TYPE 10 TO TYPE 251 ROAD TEST PORTFOLIO
BUGATTI TYPE 41 TO TYPE 55 ROAD TEST PORTFOLIO
BUGATTI TYPE 57 TO TYPE 251 ROAD TEST PORTFOLIO
DELAHAYE ROAD TEST PORTFOLIO
FERRARI ROAD CARS 1946-1956 ROAD TEST PORTFOLIO
FIAT 500 1936-1972 ROAD TEST PORTFOLIO
FIAT DINO ROAD TEST PORTFOLIO
HISPANO SUIZA ROAD TEST PORTFOLIO
HONDA ST1100/ST1300 PAN EUROPEAN 1990-2002 RTP
JAGUAR MK1 & MK2 ROAD TEST PORTFOLIO
LOTUS CORTINA ROAD TEST PORTFOLIO
MV AGUSTA F4 750 & 1000 1997-2007 ROAD TEST PORTFOLIO
TATRA CARS ROAD TEST PORTFOLIO

VELOCEPRESS MOTORCYCLE BOOKS & MANUALS

AJS SINGLES & TWINS 250cc THRU 1000cc 1932-1948 (BOOK OF)
AJS SINGLES 1955-65 350cc & 500cc (BOOK OF)
AJS SINGLES 1945-60 350cc & 500cc MODELS 16 & 18 (BOOK OF)
ARIEL 1939-1960 4 STROKE SINGLES (BOOK OF)
ARIEL LEADER & ARROW 1958-1964 (BOOK OF)
ARIEL MOTORCYCLES 1933-1951 WSM
ARIEL PREWAR MODELS 1932-1939 (BOOK OF)
BMW M/CYCLES R26 R27 (1956-1967) FACTORY WSM
BMW M/CYCLES R50 R50S R60 R69S (1955-1969) FACTORY WSM
BSA BANTAM (BOOK OF)
BSA ALL FOUR-STROKE SINGLES & V-TWINS 1936-1952 (BOOK OF)
BSA OHV & SV SINGLES - 250cc 1954-1970 (BOOK OF)
BSA OHV & SV SINGLES 1945-54 250-600cc (BOOK OF)
BSA OHV SINGLES 350 & 500cc 1955-1967 (BOOK OF)
BSA PRE-WAR MODELS TO 1939 (BOOK OF)
BSA TWINS 1948-1962 (BOOK OF)
BSA TWINS 1962-1969 (SECOND BOOK OF)
CATALOG OF BRITISH MOTORCYCLES (1951 MODELS)
DOUGLAS PRE-WAR ALL MODELS 1929-1939 (BOOK OF)
DOUGLAS POST-WAR ALL MODELS 1948-1957 FACTORY WSM
DUCATI 160cc, 250cc & 350cc OHC MODELS FACTORY WSM
HONDA 50 ALL MODELS UP TO 1970 INC MONKEY & TRAIL (BOOK OF)
HONDA 90 ALL MODELS UP TO 1966 (BOOK OF)
HONDA MOTORCYCLES 125-150 TWINS C/CS/CB/CA WSM
HONDA MOTORCYCLES 250-305 TWINS C/CS/CB WSM
HONDA MOTORCYCLES C100 SUPER CUB WSM
HONDA MOTORCYCLES C110 SPORT CUB 1962-1969 WSM
HONDA TWINS & SINGLES 50cc THRU 305cc 1960-1966 (BOOK OF)
HONDA TWINS & SINGLES 125cc THRU 450cc UP TO 1968 (BOOK OF)
INDIAN PONYBIKE, BOY RACER & PAPOOSE ILL PARTS LIST & SALES LIT
J.A.P. ENGINES 1927-1952 & MOTORCYCLES 1934-1952 (BOOK OF)
LAMBRETTA ALL 125 & 150cc MODELS 1947-1957 (BOOK OF)
LAMBRETTA LI & TV MODELS 1957-1970 (SECOND BOOK OF)
MATCHLESS 350 & 500cc SINGLES 1945-1956 (BOOK OF)
MATCHLESS 350 & 500cc SINGLES 1955-1966 (BOOK OF)
NORTON 1932-1947 (BOOK OF)
NORTON 1938-1956 (BOOK OF)
NORTON DOMINATOR TWINS 1955-1965 (BOOK OF)
NORTON MODELS 19, 50 & E52 1955-1963 (BOOK OF)
NORTON MOTORCYCLES 1957-1970 FACTORY WSM
NORTON PREWAR MODELS 1932-1939 (BOOK OF)
NSU PRIMA ALL MODELS 1956-1964 (BOOK OF)
NSU QUICKLY ALL MODELS 1953-1963 (BOOK OF)
RALEIGH MOPEDS 1960-1969 (BOOK OF)
ROYAL ENFIELD SINGLES & V TWINS 1934-1946 (BOOK OF)
ROYAL ENFIELD SINGLES & V TWINS 1937-1953 (BOOK OF)
ROYAL ENFIELD SINGLES 1946-1962 (BOOK OF)
ROYAL ENFIELD 736cc INTERCEPTOR FACTORY WSM
ROYAL ENFIELD 250cc & 350cc SINGLES 1958-1966 (SECOND BOOK OF)
SUNBEAM MOTORCYCLES 1928-1939 (BOOK OF)
SUNBEAM S7 & S8 1946-1957 (BOOK OF)
SUZUKI 50cc & 80cc UP TO 1966 (BOOK OF)
SUZUKI T10 1963-1967 FACTORY WSM
SUZUKI T20 & T200 1965-1969 FACTORY WSM
TRIUMPH PRE-WAR MOTORCYCLE 1935-1939 (BOOK OF)
TRIUMPH MOTORCYCLES 1935-1949 (BOOK OF)
TRIUMPH MOTORCYCLES 1937-1951 WSM
TRIUMPH MOTORCYCLES 1945-1955 FACTORY WSM
TRIUMPH TWINS 1945-1958 (BOOK OF)
TRIUMPH TWINS 1956-1969 (BOOK OF)
VELOCETTE ALL SINGLES & TWINS 1925-1970 (BOOK OF)
VESPA 1951-1961 (BOOK OF)
VESPA 125 & 150cc & GS MODELS 1955-1963 (SECOND BOOK OF)
VESPA 90, 125 & 150cc 1963-1972 (THIRD BOOK OF)
VESPA GS & SS 1955-1968 (BOOK OF)
VILLIERS ENGINE (BOOK OF)
VINCENT MOTORCYCLES 1935-1955 WSM

PLEASE VISIT OUR WEBSITE
www.VelocePress.com
FOR A DETAILED DESCRIPTION
OF ANY OF THESE TITLES

www.ingramcontent.com/pod-product-compliance
Lightning Source LLC
Chambersburg PA
CBHW070553170426
43201CB00012B/1833